TEPOZTLÁN

Village in Mexico

BY

OSCAR LEWIS

University of Illinois

CASE STUDIES IN CULTURAL ANTHROPOLOGY

HOLT, RINEHART AND WINSTON
NEW YORK   CHICAGO   SAN FRANCISCO   TORONTO   LONDON

Copyright © 1960
by Holt, Rinehart and Winston, Inc.
Library of Congress Catalog Card Number: 60-7330

03-006050-8

Printed in the United States of America
90123   3   1918171615141312

CASE STUDIES IN
CULTURAL ANTHROPOLOGY

GENERAL EDITORS

George and Louise Spindler

STANFORD UNIVERSITY

TEPOZTLÁN

Village in Mexico

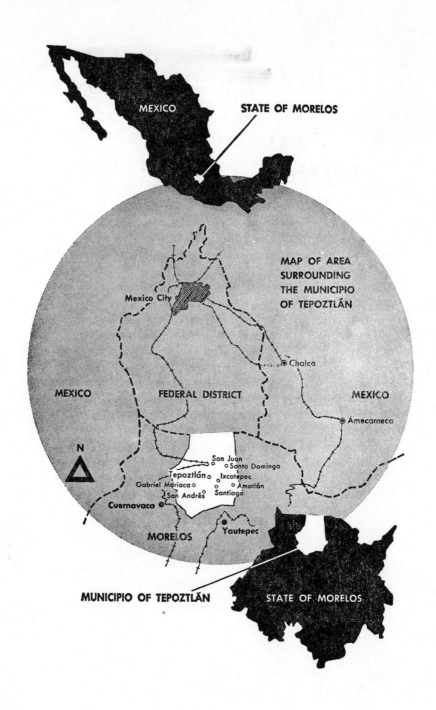

MEXICO

STATE OF MORELOS

MAP OF AREA
SURROUNDING
THE MUNICIPIO
OF TEPOZTLÁN

Mexico City

Chalco

MEXICO

FEDERAL DISTRICT

MEXICO

Amecameca

N

San Juan
Santo Domingo
Tepoztlán   Ixcatepec
Gabriel Mariaca   Amatlán
San Andrés   Santiago
Cuernavaca

MORELOS   Yautepec

MUNICIPIO OF TEPOZTLÁN

STATE OF MORELOS

About the Author

OSCAR LEWIS holds a Ph.D. from Columbia University and is at present professor of anthropology at the University of Illinois. He was a consulting anthropologist for the Ford Foundation in 1952-54 and a Guggenheim Fellow in 1956-57. He has done fieldwork with Blackfoot Indians and Texas farmers, and in Spain, Cuba, and India, as well as in Mexico, where he has studied Mexican peasant culture intermittently since 1943. Among his books are *Village Life in Northern India, Life in a Mexican Village: Tepoztlán Restudied,* and *Five Families: Mexican Case Studies in the Culture of Poverty.*

About the Book

This is a book of very broad scope about a single Mexican village. Tepoztlán, the village, is placed on a time line that extends from the tenth century A.D. and the Toltec Empire, to the present; from legendary history to contemporary anthropological observation. The main focus of the book is upon life as it is lived today in this village, typical of many, by the Mexican peasant. Economics, intrafamily relationships, and the life cycle are described. Dr. Lewis analyzes the inner feelings of the villagers, their motivations and values, and in the last chapter gives us a vivid account of change as Tepoztlán acquires electricity, new roads, buses — and even formulas for bottle babies; all harbingers of more sweeping changes to come as the village of the Mexican peasant adapts to the impact of urbanization and industrialization.

GEORGE AND LOUISE SPINDLER
General Editors

Stanford, California
December 1959

Acknowledgments

I thank the University of Illinois Press for their kind permission to utilize materials published in my earlier volume *Life in a Mexican Village: Tepoztlán Restudied* (1951). To Alberto Beltrán I am grateful for the drawings of village scenes. I am also grateful to the Guggenheim Foundation for a Fellowship which made possible my second restudy of the village in 1956-57.

Contents

Introduction

ONE OF THE major trends in cultural anthropology during the last twenty years has been a shift from the study of isolated tribal peoples to the study of peasantry in the economically underdeveloped countries. The village of Tepoztlán, in Mexico, is especially interesting in this connection because it was one of the first peasant communities to be studied by an American anthropologist. Robert Redfield worked in the village in 1926-27 and in 1930 published *Tepoztlán—a Mexican Village*. Seventeen years later, in 1943, I restudied the village and in 1951 published *Life in a Mexican Village: Tepoztlán Restudied*. In 1956-57 I returned to Tepoztlán to learn what changes had taken place since my earlier work. In all, I have spent approximately three years of field work in the village since 1943. Few peasant communities have been studied more intensively by independent investigators. Moreover, the combination of archeological data, historical archive material dating from the sixteenth century, and three anthropological studies spread over a thirty-year period has given us an unusual time perspective for the study of culture change.

Tepoztlán may be designated as a peasant society in the sense that it has an old and stable population, the villagers have a great attachment to the land, agriculture is the major source of livelihood, the technology is relatively primitive (hoe and plow), and production is primarily for subsistence, with barter persisting, although the people also participate in a money economy. Moreover, the village is integrated into larger political units such as the state and the nation and is subject to their laws. The villagers pay taxes, send their children to school, and vote in national and state elections. Tepoztlán has also been exposed to urban influences and has borrowed from other rural areas as well as from urban centers, but it has managed to integrate the new traits into a relatively stable culture pattern. Finally, the community is poor, has a high incidence of illiteracy and a high birth and death rate, and has been under foreign domination for long periods of time. Thus it has developed that peculiar combination of dependence on and hostility toward government which is so characteristic of peasants and colonial peoples.

1

Since a peasant village is by definition part of a larger society, usually the nation, it becomes important to understand it within the national context and to determine how national institutions and national history affect it. On the other hand, a study of a single village in a predominantly agricultural country can give us insight into many aspects of the nation as a whole. For example, Tepoztlán mirrors many national trends and brings into sharp focus some of the most pressing problems of Mexico. The changes which have oc-curred in Tepoztlán since the Revolution—the introduction of corn mills, the granting of *ejidos* to some of the landless (see p. 27), the building of a modern highway, the establishment of bus service, the expansion of educational facilities —are typical of changes which are taking place over wide areas in Mexico. Similarly, many of the problems which stand out in Tepoztlán can be seen in thousands of Mexican villages—for example, the poor agricultural resources, population pressure, the importance of forest and grazing lands in the agri-cultural economy, soil erosion, deforestation, the small size of land holdings, low yields, and the absence of adequate credit facilities. One advantage in studying these problems within the framework of a single village is that we can clearly see the interrelationship between geographic, historic, economic, social, political, and psychological factors.

Tepoztlán also reflects to a remarkable degree many of the character-istics of Mexico as a whole. Within the relatively limited area of the *municipio* (county) of Tepoztlán we find practically the entire range of the various climatic zones of Mexico—from the *tierra fría* (cold country) to the *tierra caliente* (hot tropical country)—and their accompanying variety of natural resources. Over 50 percent of the total land area of Mexico falls within the range of altitudes found within this single municipio—that is, from approxi-mately 3,500 to 9,500 feet. The statistical indices of Tepoztlán also follow national figures for such items as the percentage of forest land to total land and the average size of landholding. In addition, the rate of population growth as well as the distribution of age groups closely parallels national figures for the rural population.

In Tepoztlán, as in Mexico as a whole, there are contrasting elements of the primitive and the modern, the Spanish colonial and the contemporary. Tepoztlán has a strong Indian heritage; many pre-Hispanic traits have per-sisted and are found in the village today. The system of communal landowner-ship and the social organization of the municipio have remained practically intact for the past four hundred years. Many elements of pre-Hispanic agricul-ture are found; corn, beans, and squash remain the staple crops. Pre-Hispanic traits of material culture have also persisted, particularly in house construction, furnishings, cookery, and clothing. Among the more important of these items are adobe walls, the sweat house made of stone and mortar, clay-plastered granaries for corn, the hearth, the three-legged grinding stone, the clay griddle, the mortar and pestle, huaraches, chile, and *pulque*. In nonmaterial culture the survivals are found especially in curing and magic and in the customs per-taining to birth and other stages of the life cycle. The Nahuatl language has been retained. As late as 1927 Nahuatl was spoken by nearly all the villagers, although most of them also spoke Spanish.

The large number of Spanish colonial elements which still exist in the village culture were introduced early in the sixteenth century, soon after the Spanish conquest. The most important of these traits are the physical layout of the village with its barrios, streets, and central plaza; Catholicism and the churches; the Spanish language; a money economy; domestic animals; the plow and other agricultural tools; and the greater part of the beliefs and customs of the people.

Side by side with the pre-Hispanic and Spanish colonial elements are many significant items of modern industrial civilization. These include corn mills and sewing machines, a modern highway and buses, clocks, poolrooms, patent medicines, powdered milk, battery radios, and a few automobiles. The existence of both old and new traits and the varying degree in which they are combined from family to family creates cultural complexity and heterogeneity in Tepoztlán.

It is important also to consider how Tepoztlán is distinctive. If we compare it with other villages in Mexico rather than with the nation as a whole, we find that it is atypical in many ways. Tepoztlán is larger than 90 percent of the villages of Mexico and has a greater complexity of social organization. Unlike many other municipios, Tepoztlán has retained its communal lands, and specialized industries are absent or have disappeared. The proximity of the village to Mexico City and to Cuernavaca has exposed it to new ideas. It has a long tradition of literacy with a local intelligentsia which has existed since the 1850's. Moreover, at various times in the history of the village Tepoztecans have achieved positions of prominence in different fields and have had personal contacts with men in the highest political circles of the state of Morelos and of the nation. In the middle of the last century many young men of the well-to-do class left Tepoztlán to become doctors, lawyers, teachers, engineers, and priests. The village boasts of having produced within the last fifty years two governors of the state of Morelos, three justices in the state court, a senator, and more than half a dozen deputies to the state legislature. These men or their descendants have kept in touch with their relatives in the village and so have been a constant stimulus for culture change.

The first seven chapters of this book describe Tepoztlán as it appeared to me between 1943 and 1948 and are based upon my earlier study, *Life in a Mexican Village: Tepoztlán Restudied.* The reader may refer to the earlier volume for detailed references to source material and the methodology employed. Chapter 8 of this book describes the village as of 1956.

I

The Setting

TEPOZTLÁN is an ancient highland village in the state of Morelos, about sixty miles south of Mexico City. It has been continuously inhabited at least since the time of Christ. It is the administrative head of the municipio of Tepoztlán which embraces an area of 60,000 acres and consists of eight villages. The village of Tepoztlán is centrally located within the municipio and nestles in a broad alluvial valley surrounded by beautiful buttes or cliffs which rise to 1,200 feet above the house sites. The cliffs or *cerros* form a natural fortress and at various times have served as a refuge for the villagers. Each *cerro* is known to the villagers by its ancient Nahuatl name and each has a legend associated with it. One of the cliffs has been an important archeological site since 1895 when a stone temple of a Tepoztecan deity was unearthed. The temple and the great scenic beauty of the village have begun to attract tourists in recent years.

The location of Tepoztlán in an intermediate position between the *tierra fría* and the *tierra caliente* gives it an excellent temperate climate. The climate is one of the most healthful in the state of Morelos, and Tepoztlán has one of the lowest death rates in the state. Tepoztlán is just above the malaria area and although malaria occurs, it is generally contracted by villagers who have been working in the lowlands to the south.

The average annual rainfall in the village is about 60 inches, most of which comes during the rainy season beginning in May or early June and generally lasting until early September. The dry season begins in October or November and lasts for seven long months. Because of the dry season only one crop a year can be grown. Lack of water for irrigation is one of the most frequent complaints made by the villagers, who speak of the irrigated farming area of Yautepec, where several crops a year are grown, as an agricultural paradise.

There are twenty-six public fountains in the village to which water is piped from a spring in one of the *cerros*. Most of the fountains are made of clay and cement; some are semienclosed, protected by a roof, and topped by

4

a cross; others are merely open tanks. Although hauling water has been the traditional and common practice, it is now considered a hardship by more and more families.

A rich semitropical flora grows in the village. On almost any house site a great variety of plants and trees are found: papaya, coffee, hog plum (*ciruela*), *guaje,* avocado, *chayote,* mango, banana, maguey, and some prickly pear. Most families grow a variety of flowers and herbs which they use for cooking and as medicines.

Tepoztlán is located on a slope, the northern or upper part of the village being several hundred feet higher than the southern part. The upper part is steeper, rockier, and somewhat cooler, while the lower part is better watered and has a richer flora. The streets running north and south slope steeply and during the rainy season they often become cascading streams. To avoid erosion, many streets have been stone paved and terraced according to the Aztec system of terracing, which involves a series of alternating slopes and levels. Only the paved road and the plaza in the center are on a more or less level plane.

The village is large, sprawling, roughly rectangular in shape, and approximately a mile and a fourth in length and a mile in width. Although it contains 662 house sites, it does not have the compact or crowded appearance of some Mexican towns since for the most part the houses are separated from each other by gardens, corrals, or small *milpas.* The stone walls which enclose the house sites are low, do not block the view from the street, and permit overhanging trees to shade the street. Only a few houses in the center of the village are built contiguously in Spanish style and are enclosed by high, concealing walls.

Tepoztlán has a typical Mexican plaza complete with park, bandstand, shade trees, and benches. Around the plaza are grouped the chief buildings: courthouse, offices for the president, secretary, and other local officials, the schoolhouse, the main church, some stores, a grain mill, and a small marketing center. This central part of the village has the appearance and some of the hustle of a town, but it does not give the impression of a thriving community. The park, plaza, and public buildings show evidence of chronic neglect; only for the annual *carnaval* is the area well swept and the main fountain cleaned. The villagers seldom use the park, and it is usually abandoned except when there are tourists. The stores are small and dark with unattractive displays. On market days the few vendors and the small variety of goods for sale betray the lack of commercial activity.

The streets off the center are uniformly rustic and quiet and stamp Tepoztlán as a rural village. The names of only those streets nearest the plaza are indicated by placards. As is customary in Mexico, street names commemorate important historical events and outstanding local figures; some are in Nahuatl and refer to pre-Hispanic figures. Again, only the houses in the center are numbered, although not in any systematic order. Street names or house numbers are not used by the villagers in speaking or writing, nor do they appear on letters mailed in from the outside.

At night the village appears even more rustic because of the absence of public street lighting. When there is no moon it is difficult—even dangerous—to walk through the rough streets without a flashlight or candle, and usually only young men venture out at night. The only sounds are those of the animals, the serenades of romantic youths, and an occasional drunken peasant being taken home. Even during the day the village is not noisy, although many sounds may be heard: voices from within the houses, children crying or playing, housewives slapping tortillas into shape, people and animals walking over the stones, church bells, buses racing and honking along the main thoroughfare, and an occasional lone peddler crying his wares.

Population

The population of Tepoztlán, like that of Mexico as a whole, has shown a rapid increase in recent years. The village had a population of 3,230 according to the census of 1940; by 1947 it numbered well over 4,000. One of the causal factors for the rise was the sharp decline in mortality rates, especially for infants, during the period from 1930 to 1940. This decline, in turn, was caused by the increase and greater availability of medical services and the fairly intensive program of inoculation carried out by the Mexican Department of Health. Since 1930 there have been doctors in residence in the village for short periods, and some villagers visit private doctors and the free health clinic in Cuernavaca. Five mid-wives with some training in modern hygienic methods now live in the village. The longer life span of the villagers (15.5 percent of Tepoztecans are people over fifty as compared to 9.9 percent for all rural Mexico) is probably related to an increasingly higher standard of living in the village as well as to its healthful climate.

Language and Literacy

Two languages are spoken in Tepoztlán, Spanish and the indigenous Nahuatl. In 1920 nearly all the villagers spoke Nahuatl, but since that time there has been a marked decrease in its use, with a corresponding increase in the use of Spanish. About one-half of the villagers are still bilingual, but in 1944 there were only five persons who spoke Nahuatl alone. Nahuatl is still preferred at barrio meetings and for the ceremonial address at some fiestas. The bus companies have Nahuatl names, and in sports events the competitors will sometimes take Nahuatl names.

The younger generation has a distinctly negative attitude toward Nahuatl; people under thirty-five tend to be ashamed of speaking it in the presence of outsiders and frequently deny having any knowledge of it. Within most homes, members of the older generation customarily speak in Spanish but resort to Nahuatl to tell secrets and jokes and to express themselves more emphatically when they are quarreling. Thus many children have come to associate speaking Nahuatl with quarreling and scolding.

The greater use of Spanish in the village has not been accompanied by an equal increase in literacy. In 1940, 42 percent of the villagers could not read or write. In general there is a high correlation between membership in the middle economic group and literacy; many in the upper economic group are illiterate. The reading of newspapers has increased considerably in recent years. In 1920 no newspapers came regularly to the village, while in 1944 fifty-six people bought newspapers on an average of twice a week. These people have played an important role in determining village opinion on local, national, and international issues.

Means of Communication

With a modern highway, bus service, mail service, some telephones, telegraph, and a nearby railroad, Tepoztlán has relatively good means of communication. The railroad, built about 1900, encouraged the commercial exploitation of natural resources and is now used chiefly to transport wood and charcoal to Mexico City. Before the highway, communication between the village and surrounding regions was by burro and by foot, and most trading and social contacts were with the nearby town of Yautepec. With the coming of the road and the bus lines, Cuernavaca replaced Yautepec in importance. Because of the cultural sophistication of Cuernavaca, this shift accelerated the rate of change in Tepoztlán. The village has had mail service since 1926, and mail is delivered daily. It has had the telephone and telegraph since before the Revolution, but until recently they have been either out of order or used only infrequently.

Housing and House Furnishings

The houses of Tepoztlán consist essentially of three types: the flimsy *jacal*, the adobe house, and the more substantial dwellings found in the center of the village. The *jacal* and the adobe house are basically Indian, while the houses in the center show Spanish influence.

The *jacal*, the poorest type of house, and considered primitive and undesirable by the majority of the villagers, is constructed of cornstalks or Mexican bamboo (*otate*) and has a thatched roof and an earthen floor. Only 5 percent of the dwellings are of this type, and they are limited to the smaller, outlying areas, particularly the upper part of the village. According to the Mexican Housing Census of 1939, the *jacal* makes up 38.7 percent of all dwellings in the Central Mesa region in which Tepoztlán is located and the percentage for all Mexico is 44.9. These figures indicate a comparatively high standard of housing in Tepoztlán.

The great majority of Tepoztecan families (approximately 90 percent) are housed in the more solid adobe, tile-roofed houses. These sometimes have brick floors but more usually earthen ones, and consist of one or more rectangular rooms each of which generally has only one opening, a doorway. Some of the newer adobe houses have wooden-shuttered window openings as well. The door of each room opens directly onto the yard or porch rather than into other rooms in the interior of the house. Frequently, as families grow larger, additional sleeping rooms are built, and many families add a kitchen in the form of a bamboo lean-to with a tile roof.

In sharp contrast with the *jacal* and adobe houses, the few homes of the wealthier families of the center barrios show marked Spanish or modern urban influence, and several of them border on elegance. They are built of brick or stone, covered with plaster, and whitewashed inside and out. Large and imposing, they are surrounded by a high outer wall which is built flush with the street and in which glass-paned windows and small balconies of iron grillwork are set.

Although only the poorest live in *jacales,* it is by no means true that the wealthiest live in the finest houses. Families of every category of wealth live in simple adobe houses, and a few of the richest men who represent the conservative older generation continue to live in relatively unimproved houses. Newly rich families also tend to build homes with a simple exterior even though the interior may have a degree of elegance. The destruction wreaked against the homes of the *caciques* during the Revolution is well remembered, and there still exists some fear on the part of Tepoztecans of acquiring a reputation of being wealthy.

The great majority of the houses in Tepoztlán have no running water or sanitary facilities of any kind. A few families near the center have water piped directly into their patios or kitchens, a privilege for which they pay a small tax to the municipio. No attempt has been made to control this private use of the public water supply, however, and some persons with such a supply permit relatives, friends, or *compadres* to take as much water as they wish, or even allow a neighbor to connect his pipe to theirs to avoid paying the tax. Invariably the few families with private water have flourishing orchards and gardens. Sometimes the uncontrolled private use greatly decreases the flow of water into the nearest public fountain, particularly during the dry season. Conflict has often been the result. Not infrequently, private water pipes are deliberately stuffed up or damaged by less fortunate neighbors, and sometimes groups of angry residents, headed by a political leader, break into houses to cut off the private water supply that is draining the public one.

The benefits of toilets are not generally recognized: only one private house and the two tourist homes have toilets that can be flushed. The new schoolhouse, however, has toilets and showers, and the younger generation is becoming accustomed to them. Bathing facilities for women and children consist of a small clay or tin basin used in the home, although many women bathe and wash their hair when they do their laundry in a stream or at the public washing place. The men and older boys bathe in the river.

No Tepoztecan house has any means of heating other than the kitchen fire. This gives little heat and, moreover, it is extinguished as soon as cooking is completed, in order to save fuel. In the winter the villagers generally retire early to keep warm, but since most families have few blankets they suffer from cold during winter nights. Of the various means of lighting the houses after dark, the most common and inexpensive is the candle. Some houses have kerosene lamps, and the stores and a few of the houses in the center have Coleman gasoline lamps. One house—that of a prosperous curer—has electricity which is supplied by his own generator.

Differences in house furnishings are even more striking than differences in house types. As an example of the unending variety of combinations of modern and primitive household items, it is not at all unusual to find a battery-operated radio, a pre-Hispanic hearth as the only means of cooking, a hand mill for grinding coffee, and the Indian stone *metate* for grinding corn, all under one roof. Some of the youth, the more educated, and the middle economic group, have a strong desire to live better and to invest in household comforts—in modern equipment for cooking, sleeping, and lighting. Most members of the older generation, however—even those with means—scorn innovations and prefer to live the way they have always lived, investing what surplus they have in land and cattle. Thus the use of modern household equipment correlates more with age and education than with wealth, and such equipment is found most frequently in the homes of families with a medium income. But the homes of the better-to-do almost always contain a greater quantity of household goods, whether primitive or modern.

Almost every house has a hearth, either on the floor or raised to almost table height by means of a cement platform. The *comal* (griddle) for toasting tortillas may be of clay or iron, but with the increasing consumption of bread the griddle is used less than formerly. The same is true of the *metate* (grinding stone), since almost all women now have their corn ground at the mill. Nevertheless, no Tepoztecan woman sets up housekeeping without her own *metate* for regrinding corn, for grinding coffee and large quantities of chile for fiestas, and for emergencies.

The remaining house furnishings are relatively few—mainly sleeping equipment, religious articles, and various containers for storage. The beds are of three kinds: the *petate* or straw mat placed on the floor; the *tepexco,* a raised bed of bamboo sticks tied together and placed on a wooden frame or on two sawhorses; and a brass or iron bedstead with metal springs over which a *petate,* rather than a mattress, generally is placed. The great majority of the villagers sleep either on the floor or on the *tepexco;* only about 20 percent sleep on a bed or cot. For Mexico as a whole, the proportion of those who sleep on a bed or cot is far greater (61 percent) and even for communities of 10,000 or fewer inhabitants it is 53 percent. Most Tepoztecans sleep on the floor because they cannot afford to buy beds, but the older people sleep on the floor by preference, feeling that it is safer, makes them less subject to *los aires* (evil winds), or is more comfortable. Pillows, mattresses, bed linen, and bedspreads are found in only a few Tepoztecan homes. A wool *serape* is all the bedding known to most.

Sleeping arrangements vary from family to family, but the most widespread custom is for children of from about two to six to sleep between their parents on the *petate* A nursing baby sleeps on the outside, next to his mother. Cradles are used only during the day. Older children sleep apart, the girls sharing one *petate* and the boys another. In homes with two rooms, the parents and small children sleep in one room and the older children in the other. Few homes have enough rooms to permit the separation of older brothers and sisters. Sometimes parents are embarrassed to lie down together in the presence of their children; the mother then sleeps with the daughters while the father sleeps with the sons.

Most homes have a makeshift altar in the main room of the house. This is usually a table, frequently covered with tissue paper, on which are placed candles, flowers, incense burners, and statues of the saints. Religious pictures are hung on the wall over the table.

Less than a dozen battery-operated radios and about forty-four spring-driven phonographs are owned by the villagers. In 1943 there were 215 sewing machines in Tepoztlán. These machines were owned by 25 percent of the families but they serviced many more than that number since it is customary to lend or rent them to relatives and neighbors. Most machines are in continuous use. Indeed it may be said that one of the secondary, although not unimportant, effects of the sewing machine has been to provide the women with an excuse for visiting each other, thereby extending their social life.

Diet

As in rural Mexico as a whole, the basic diet of the people of Tepoztlán consists of corn, beans, and chile, the proportion of the three staples to other foods varying sharply from family to family according to season, income, and food habits. In general, the poorer the family, the higher the consumption of the three staples as compared to meat, milk, bread, cheese, and other foods. Corn is the major food, ranging from 10 to as much as 70 percent of a family's diet.

Corn is most frequently eaten in the form of tortillas, occasionally as *atole* (gruel). At certain fiestas, tamales made of corn dough are eaten. A wide variety of beans is found in Tepoztlán, the most common being red kidney beans which are cooked with lard, chile, and sometimes tomato and onion. Green chile, ground with onion and tomato, is daily made into a sauce to be eaten with the tortillas and whatever other foods are served.

The basic diet is supplemented by other foods which are locally cultivated, gathered wild, or purchased in the stores and market place. Those locally produced include banana, orange, lemon, lime, grapefruit, hog plum, papaya, mango, prickly pear, avocado, squash, tomato, *zapote, chayote, manzanillos, pitos,* acacia seeds, sugar cane, *chirimoya, mameys,* peanuts, coffee, honey, spices, herbs, beef, pork, chicken, turkey, milk, eggs, cheese, and clotted cream. The fields, forests, and mountainsides provide several varieties of wild edible greens the year round. These are not considered a desirable food, but they are important because they provide food elements which the Tepoztecan diet would otherwise lack. During times of scarcity a large number of families eat wild greens in quantity several times a week; the chronically poor eat them regularly throughout the year.

Foods bought in the stores of Tepoztlán, Yautepec, Cuernavaca, or Mexico City are bread, sugar, salt, rice, certain types of chile and beans, noodles, and dried codfish. Chocolate is used but is considered a luxury. Evaporated and powdered milk, canned sardines, tomato herring, and other fish are used by a small minority but are slowly becoming more popular.

The eating of white bread made of wheat flour is of particular interest in Mexico since it is a relatively new trait and one which has been taken to indicate the degree of acculturation both of individuals and of groups. In Tepoztlán, bread is considered a very desirable food, and the social and economic status of a family is often judged in terms of the amount of bread it consumes. In 1940 over 31 percent of the villagers ate bread fairly regularly; three years later there was hardly a family that did not eat bread even though it may have been only once or twice a month. Bread is especially favored as a food for small children; even the poorest family tries to provide a piece of bread for its youngest child every day. There is no indication, however, that bread will eventually displace the tortilla, for even among the well-to-do families bread consumption represents at most about 10 percent of the total food expenditure.

There is, of course, much variation in the actual consumption of food. Except among the wealthier families, irregularity in diet is characteristic throughout the year; few families maintain a uniformly good diet from day to day even by local standards. The leanest season of the year is the three or four months preceding the harvest when many families are reduced to minimum quantities of tortilla, beans, and chile. Before fiestas, money is needed for new clothes, for the fiesta meal, and for other expenses. Many families pull in their belts at this time and eat less in order to sell their corn, beans, eggs, and chickens for cash. The best eating occurs just after harvest and on fiesta days when *mole,* made with chicken or turkey, and rice and beans are prepared. Other irregularities of consumption are caused by the seasonal availability of fruits and vegetables. If the family trees produce poor or little fruit, for example, the family goes without fruit.

Meat consumption rises during the dry winter months when pasture is scarce, for cattle are then slaughtered. Eggs are generally eaten only by the men, especially during the planting season when work is intense. Chicken and turkey are delicacies reserved for fiestas, weddings, baptisms, and birthdays. With the exception of the wedding feast, which is socially obligatory and served by rich and poor alike, many families must forego fiesta meals, sometimes for years on end, and partake of them only when invited by other families. Game is not eaten extensively; the few men who hunt do so only when, as in the dry season, there is no other work.

Differences in the diet of the rich and poor are principally differences in the amount of food eaten and in the relative frequency with which a family can afford to eat the more desirable of the locally known food types. There are no class differences in food quality, in food types, and in ways of preparing dishes. It is commonly said in Tepoztlán that the rich are too miserly to eat any better than the poor. Not wealth as such, but education or degree of acculturation is now beginning to create real differences in diet.

Tepoztecan families normally eat three meals a day, although many remember eating only twice a day before and during the Revolution. The entire family seldom eats together and often there are no fixed hours for meals. The father and older sons have breakfast together in the morning before they go to the fields; if the fields are at a great distance they carry their breakfast with them, to be warmed and eaten later. They may eat in the fields again at noon and have their dinner when they arrive home, at any time between 5 and 9 P.M. When they eat at home they usually are served first. The mother serves them, handing each person his food in a bowl or rolled in a tortilla.

The women and the children eat breakfast at 7 or 8 A.M., dinner at about 1 P.M., and supper at dusk. Usually the younger children are fed before the mother and the older daughters sit down to eat. In most homes the men sit on low chairs or stools and the women and children sit on the floor. Very few families use a table except for a fiesta meal and then only for the men and guests. Likewise, knives and forks, if used at all, are reserved for guests at fiesta time. Spoons are sometimes used, but usually food is eaten with the tortilla as a spoon.

Like most Mexicans, Tepoztecans believe that food can be classified as "hot" and "cold," a classification which has no relationship to the temperature or the flavor of the foods. (Ice cream, for example, is classified as "hot," while most meats are called "cold.") In general, "cold" foods are believed to cause diarrhea and to be less easily digested than "hot" foods. They are therefore not given to very small children or to women who have just given birth. During certain illnesses, only "hot" foods should be eaten; during others only "cold" foods. Foods may be neutralized—that is, made less dangerous—by mixing certain "hot" foods with certain "cold" foods. Tepoztecans are not meticulous about following the rules, however, nor do they always agree what the rules are or how a food, particularly a new food, should be classified.

Clothing

Both old and new styles of clothes are worn in Tepoztlán—age, occupation, and, to a limited degree, economic status being the factors which determine the style preferred. The old-type clothing is essentially Spanish in origin with some admixture and adaptation from pre-Hispanic times. For women it consists of a long dark-colored skirt, a white underskirt, a collarless undershirt, a high-necked blouse, a half-apron, a sash, and a *rebozo*. The old-type clothing for men consists of white cloth pants (*calzones*), long white cotton underdrawers, white undershirt, a white collarless overshirt, a white cotton jacket, leather huaraches, and a straw sombrero. The *serape,* an important article of clothing, is used for warmth and for protection against rain.

The new type of dress was worn by the wealthier and more sophisticated Tepoztecans in the 1920's, but since that time members of all socio-economic levels have adopted it. For women it includes a one-piece dress, a full-length slip, and a long apron. Unmarried girls wear underdrawers and a number of younger women have a pair of shoes and stockings for important occasions. The *rebozo* is still commonly worn, but sweaters and jackets are coming into use. Most of the changes are seen in the dress of women under forty; those over forty are more conservative and cling to the old styles.

Modern dress for men, worn mainly by the merchants, artisans, and teachers of the center, consists of dark, factory-made pants (*pantalones*), a shirt with collar and buttons, a jacket with collar, and shoes. The sombrero is sometimes replaced by a narrow-brimmed felt hat, but only the most "citified" men in Tepoztlán wear neckties. Modern dress for boys may be overalls or pants, a buttoned shirt, and a straw hat. The *serape* is now often replaced by a sweater or jacket, and many boys wear shoes. Peasants prefer the old-style dress which, they say, is cooler, cheaper, and better adapted to work in the fields.

Although clothing is becoming important as an indicator of social status, it is not necessarily an indicator of wealth. The middle economic group, rather than the upper group, tends to wear modern dress and shoes. The lowest percentage of those wearing shoes is in fact found among the wealthiest group because it is made up of the older generation.

Fiestas and Diversions

Fiestas, both religious and secular, are the major occasions for music (native drums, flageolets, and modern bands), dances, fireworks, the preparation of special dishes, rodeos, the burning of candles for a saint, flower decorations, prayer, processions, and the Mass. The fiestas serve to strengthen the *esprit de corps* of the villagers; some celebrations are joyous, others are occasions for sadness and mourning. The great majority of religious fiestas are in celebration of saints; relatively few are in celebration of Jesus or Mary.

The calendar of religious fiestas is a typical Catholic calendar which includes movable and fixed fiesta days and begins on the first of December with the opening of the season of Advent. The religious fiestas in which Tepoztecans participate are of four types: (1) the barrio fiestas in which each barrio celebrates its patron saint (see section on barrios p. 50); (2) the village-wide fiestas which celebrate the holy days in the central church; (3) the fiestas of other surrounding villages of the municipio (see municipio, p. 46); and (4) the fiestas of villages and towns outside of the municipio. Of the total of fifty-three named fiestas in which Tepoztecans participate, twenty-seven are village-wide fiestas, twelve are barrio fiestas, seven are fiestas of surrounding villages within the municipio, and seven are fiestas of villages outside of the municipio. Of the village-wide fiestas, the most important are the *carnaval*,

Ash Wednesday, the fiestas of Holy Week, the Day of *San Isidro,* the fiesta for El Tepozteco (the local culture hero) and María, the blessings of the *pericón* on September 28, the Days of the Dead, and the Days of the Posadas.

It is difficult to estimate the total number of days during a year which the villagers might devote to fiestas. Some of the fifty-three fiestas last three or four days, and a conservative estimate would be about one hundred days. It would be quite erroneous, however, to conclude that most Tepoztecans spend approximately a third of the year in fiestas, for most fiestas are attended by only a small portion of the population. Certainly less than 5 percent of the villagers attend the fourteen fiestas of the surrounding villages and other towns, and less than 10 percent attend the fiestas of barrios other than their own. There are probably less than a dozen village-wide fiestas during the year in which the village as a whole participates.

No one attends all the fiestas, but all attend some. Widows and older women are known to be great fiesta lovers and habitually attend as many as possible. The very poor tend to participate in the barrio fiestas of Tepoztlán and other villages, whereas the well-to-do are more careful to attend the religious services held in the central church. Children especially like to attend fiestas. The sharp drop in school attendance during certain fiesta times is a chronic complaint of the school. Tepoztecans also frequent the fairs of Chalma, Jiutepec, Tepalzingo, Tlayacapan, and Mazatepec. Some go to buy or sell, others go for religious devotion to a special saint, and still others go purely for diversion.

The establishment and the increasing popularity of many national holidays are encouraging a new type of sociability in the village. Unlike the traditional fiestas, these occasions are organized by the school staff and are carried out by the children. They consist of dances, plays, recitations, speeches, the singing of national songs, and parades. Occasional school dances and *kermeses,* where food and drinks are sold and games are played to raise money for various school needs, are enjoyed by the young people, but attendance is usually small because the older generation believes ballroom dancing is immoral.

Another common form of diversion is to go to Cuernavaca. On Sundays groups of young men go by bus and spend the day walking about, playing pool, drinking in the *cantinas,* and visiting prostitutes. It is the place for rendezvous, window shopping, marketing, and movie going. In short, a trip to Cuernavaca provides temporary personal freedom for Tepoztecans.

Sports as a form of recreation are limited. The traditional cockfights are all but gone and the rustic rodeos are disappearing because the young men now lack interest and skill. Hunting is seldom engaged in as a sport. Singing and serenading at night are still popular with the young men and are also a source of pleasure for most of the villagers. Organized sports or games were first introduced in Tepoztlán in 1922 during a national campaign by the Minister of Education. Baseball, soccer, volleyball, and basketball were taught by the school and had an immediate appeal. Soccer from the first was the most popular and at one time there were as many as fifteen teams. There are now five teams which play against each other and against teams from Cuernavaca and other nearby towns.

Further diversification of recreation came about with the establishment of two poolrooms in the village. Despite the pessimistic expectations of the older people, there is no evidence that the poolrooms have encouraged vice or helped to develop any new bad habits; rather they seem to have provided a harmless and much-needed diversion for the young men.

Tepoztecans have always been heavy drinkers but there are fewer habitual drunkards among them than in some of the surrounding villages. Within the last few years the price of alcohol has risen from forty centavos to five pesos a liter, a prohibitive cost which has been in part responsible for the return to the use of *pulque*. In 1942 a *pulquería* was opened in the plaza. Soft drinks such as Coca-Cola, lemonade, and other carbonated drinks are also sold in the village.

In 1939, movie equipment was installed in the school and moving pictures were shown in the village for the first time. After a month the entrepreneur moved out because of the small attendance. Two or three subsequent attempts have met with the same result, for to most Tepoztecans the admission charge of thirty or fifty centavos is prohibitive. From time to time a puppet show reaches Tepoztlán and runs for about a week. This, together with several school plays a year, makes up the theatrical entertainment.

In the past two years the church has attempted to take a more active part in providing leisure-time activities for Tepoztecans. These have included singing, presenting religious pageants and plays, celebrating saints' days, organizing religious pilgrimages, and money-making events. The new forms of entertainment have tended to make for greater differences among the various economic groups in the village, for invariably they involve an expenditure of money for dues, equipment, bus fare, clothing, or appropriate food. Thus the very poor cannot participate and continue to be limited to the fiestas and fairs.

A poor peasant's home.

2

Village History

THE HISTORY OF culture change in Tepoztlán closely follows the major divisions of Mexican history—namely, (1) the Pre-Hispanic Period; (2) the Spanish Conquest and the Colonial Period (1521) to Independence in 1810; (3) 1810 through the Díaz Regime; (4) the Revolution of 1910-20; (5) the Post-Revolutionary Period, 1920 to the present.

Pre-Hispanic Period

Tepoztlán, like Mexico, has had a long and complicated history of mingling of peoples and cultures; it has never been a truly isolated village. Its marginal position between the high plateau area to the north and the lower valleys of the south, as well as its proximity to the major roads of travel, subjected it even in pre-Hispanic times to influences from many areas. The various ceramic levels unearthed in the village show Olmec, Toltec, and Aztec influences. The village had experienced a number of conquests and had long been under political domination and authoritarian systems even before the coming of the Spaniards.

According to the legendary history of Mexico, Mixcoatl, the founder of the Toltec Empire, invaded the valley of Morelos with a Nahua horde in the early tenth century and defeated the Tlahuicas, an earlier Nahuatl-speaking people who lived in Tepoztlán. Thereafter, the Tepoztecans worshipped the benign gods of the Toltecs with offerings of paper, quail, wild pigeons, and *copal* incense. The Mexican scholar Jimenez Moreno has identified the village god El Tepozteco as the deified figure of Topiltzin, the son of Mixcoatl and a woman of Tepoztlán. Because Mixcoatl was assassinated before the birth of his son and the mother died in childbirth, Topiltzin was reared in Tepoztlán. Later he went north to avenge the death of his father by killing his kinsman, Ihuitimal.

16

The Toltec Empire was destroyed in 1246 by the Aztecs, but Tepoztlán was not involved until 1437 when Moctezuma Ilhuicomina captured it. The village was under Aztec domination for about one hundred years, probably as a semiautonomous seignory like Cuernavaca and Yautepec. To its Aztec rulers Tepoztlán paid tribute in the form of cotton mantles, cloth, paper, pottery, shields, warrior costumes, and beans. Agricultural products made up a relatively small part of the tribute.

In this pre-Hispanic period Tepoztlán was a highly stratified society with a few lords and ruling families (*principales*) at the top of the social pyramid and the mass of commoners (*maceguales*) at the bottom. The commoners worked the lands of these rulers, built their houses, made their clothing, and gave them all they demanded. They could not deal directly with the higher lords who governed them, however, but only through the *principales* who had the position of judges. Class differences were important and pervasive and affected diet, clothing, marriage customs, and other aspects of life.

The pre-Hispanic economy was a varied one. In addition to corn production there were a number of important local industries and activities: cotton growing, weaving, paper making, lime production, and the extensive use of the maguey plant for a variety of purposes. This valuable plant provided fuel; fencing and thatching material; fibers for making sandals, rope, and cloth; gutters, files, nails, needles; and honey, sugar, vinegar, and *pulque*.

According to old legends, *pulque* was invented in or near Tepoztlán, and the villages of the municipio were famous for their celebrations and debauchery. Tepoztlán was the site of a special cult of Ometochtli (Two Rabbits), the god of *pulque*, whose fame extended throughout the Aztec Empire and made the village an important religious center. Foreigners from as far away as the kingdoms of Chiapas and Guatemala made pilgrimages there, and in certain seasons of the year the cult of Ometochtli had all the characteristics of a collective orgy. Under the Aztecs, Tepoztecans paid homage to Aztec gods and practiced the Aztec rites of human sacrifice, offering children to the rain god and the hearts of prisoners to the war god.

The Spanish Conquest and the Colonial Period to Independence, 1521-1810

Tepoztlán submitted to the conquering troops of Cortés in 1521 when they passed through the village on their way from Yautepec to Cuernavaca. Because some chieftains from Yautepec were hiding there, Cortés set fire to half the town during his one-day stay. His men reported that they found there "many pretty women and much loot." By decree of 1529 Tepoztlán was one of many villages granted to Cortés. When Cortés decided to make Cuernavaca the capital of his large estate, Tepoztlán became subject to the Correjidor of Cuernavaca and the complex administrative machinery set up by the Spanish.

Before the Conquest, the village was widely spread out. Numerous population clusters had settled along the valley near the *cerros* where there was an adequate water supply. To control the people and to facilitate taxation, the Spaniards brought together into Tepoztlán these population clusters from the outlying settlements. But in government as in other aspects of the culture, the village changed slowly, modifying rather than discarding its pre-Conquest institutions. The old hierarchal arrangements of the social structure persisted; the political and religious power was simply transferred to the new ruling group represented by the Spaniards. Moreover, many of the old *principales* were maintained in power by the Spanish conquerors. Sixteenth-century documents reveal the existence of a remarkably large government bureaucracy which included many church officials.

After the Conquest, some of the native industries, principally those concerned with the manufacture of paper and cotton cloth, expanded temporarily in response to the new market provided by the Spaniards. As late as 1575 the village was described as "swarming with workmen making paper." But in general the Conquest was a disruptive influence on local industries and caused Tepoztlán to be more and more dependent on its corn. One of the disruptive factors was the *repartimiento* system which made Tepoztlán subject to a yearly assignment of manpower for work on the haciendas, in the mines of Taxco, on construction projects in Cuernavaca and in Tepoztlán itself, and as domestic servants. In addition, Tepoztecans were required to furnish workers in emergencies. One such occasion required "400 common Indians" for the harvest of sugar cane when a hacienda ran short of Negro slaves. The villagers repeatedly complained against excessive demands for labor and begged for relief, but without success. The church and the hacienda owners worked together in exploiting Indian labor.

Tepoztlán was also subject to taxation. In the early years after the Conquest, Cortés followed the Aztec policy of collecting taxes in produce. By the latter part of the sixteenth century, however, Tepoztecans complained about making payments in kind and asked to be allowed to pay in currency. This was because the landless were forced to buy corn at exorbitant prices to pay their taxes. From 1567 on, taxes were collected both in corn and in money, an indication that the village was beginning to function as a money economy. Taxes were collected for three purposes: to provide payment to the Crown; to help support the local officials of the municipio; and to support the church and the village fiestas.

In terms of population, the Conquest and the ensuing Colonial period were drastically disruptive. The population of the municipio at the time of the Conquest was about 15,000, a figure considerably larger than at the present time or at any time after the Conquest. Sixteenth-century accounts indicate a rapid decline in the population; by 1579 the village population was 5,824 and that of the entire municipio 7,572. The major causes of the decline were epidemics, deaths in the mines of Taxco and Cuautla, and the fleeing of Tepoztecans from the municipio to avoid the high taxes. The decline continued through the colonial period; by 1807 the village population was 2,540, a drop of 56 percent in a 228 year period.

Christianity was brought to Tepoztlán with little difficulty, the poly-theism of the ancient religion permitting a relatively easy shift from the old gods to the new. According to local legend, the king Tepoztecatl realized the superiority of the new belief, willingly became a Christian, received the new name of Natividad, and allied himself with the Dominican friars in con-verting the Indians peacefully. But although the growth of Catholicism and the church in Tepoztlán was rapid, many pre-Hispanic religious elements were carried over to the new religion. The figure of Tepoztecatl retained the name of El Tepozteco along with that of Natividad and thus permanently fused old Aztec concepts with those of the Catholic church. His figure is also confused with the god Ometochtli so that today he is known both as god of the wind and as son of the Virgin Mary.

After the Conquest, the Dominicans in Tepoztlán were mainly occupied in carrying out the administrative measures of the viceroy. They also attempted to extirpate all pre-Hispanic cults, and were especially vigorous in this activity during the sixteenth century when they attacked the native priests as witches and denounced the ancient idols as instruments of the devil. They slowly suc-ceeded, as did other religious orders in Spanish America, in gathering the natives into religious associations, a move that facilitated the administrative and political functions of the colony. The church, united as it was with the state, became very strong. Church personnel were numerous and were paid from public funds, and high public officials were obliged to preside over all religious processions and ceremonies. Religious fiestas became numerous during the Colonial period, and greatly increased the church income and stimulated local trade.

Independence through the Díaz Regime, 1810-1910

The first years of Mexican independence passed almost unnoticed in Tepoztlán, where colonial forms of life continued. However, the population increased for the first time since the Conquest. By 1890 it had risen to 4,163 for the village and 8,589 for the municipio.

The first great change in Tepoztlán during this period came as a result of the Juarez Reforms of 1857, when the church and state were separated and church property was confiscated. The land belonging to the village church was distributed among a small portion of the population which became the new local aristocracy, the *caciques*. The *caciques* formed an elite who con-trolled the local government, naming the officials and prohibiting political parties and elections.

The *caciques* produced large crops on their lands, using oxen and hiring peons at eighteen centavos a day. They forbade the planting of *tlacolol* (communal lands) in order to assure a cheap labor supply for themselves. For the poor and landless it was a time of suffering and exploitation; food and goods were cheap but work was scarce and people went hungry. The poor often subsisted on herbs, mushrooms, and wild greens. Many were forced to pawn their sons as servants for from five to ten pesos a season. Debts were heavy and were passed down from father to son. When the haciendas began competing with the local *caciques* for laborers, wages rose, in some cases to as high as thirty-seven centavos a day. The recruiting agents and the overseers customarily beat peons who were unruly or who did not work quickly and those who protested were drafted into the army.

The church had reacted to the Reform laws by aggressively struggling against the liberal orientation of the Mexican government. But when Díaz came to power in 1877, the church recuperated much of its former glory. In Tepoztlán, the *caciques* supported the church as a strong conservative force and again united the church and the state. Once more, pompous religious fiestas were celebrated in the village and attendance at them was large.

A landmark in the history of Tepoztlán was the building of the railroad in 1897 through the upper part of the municipio. Although most Tepoztecans had opposed the coming of the railroad and had accused the *caciques* of selling out the communal land to the gringos, the whole population benefited from the railroad. Many villagers were hired as day laborers at three times the wages prevailing at the haciendas; trade increased, and several public works were carried out with money received by the village and municipio from the railroad company in exchange for permission to build on Tepoztecan lands. Among these were the building of the municipal building and park, the lighting of the main streets by oil lamps, and the piping of water into the village. With the railroad also came the first wire fencing and the first steel plows, and the appearance of freight trains encouraged commercial exploitation of the forests for charcoal making. The expansion of the economy at this time led to other changes. A small museum of Antiquities was founded, a public library was opened, and night classes for adults were instituted. This cultural florescence, though short-lived and limited to a small group of the well-to-do and intellectuals, earned for Tepoztlán the reputation as the Athens of Morelos.

The Revolution, 1910-20

Few villages in Mexico suffered more than Tepoztlán during the Revolution. In 1911, more than a year before Zapata's call for revolt in Morelos, Tepoztlán liberated itself by force from the rule of the local *caciques*. Later the village was the scene of repeated invasions, first by rebel troops and then by government forces, and it endured depredations at the hands of both. Cattle were killed, corn and other crops were requisitioned, women were raped or taken as hostages, and large areas of the village were burned. When the situation became even more dangerous, the villagers fled to the hills and lived there for as long as six months at a time, stealing back from time to time to pick some fruit or to bury their dead.

From the start, the villagers' sympathies were with the rebels, but only a handful understood the ideals of the Zapata movement and were motivated by them. The promise of land had great appeal, but most Tepoztecans tried to remain neutral and joined the conflict only when it became a matter of life or death. The lack of unity among the villagers became apparent in the early days of the revolt when the ablest Tepoztecan leaders killed one another in their fierce rivalry for power.

During these bitter years the religious life of the village came to a standstill. The priests and the *caciques* had fled for their lives, the church and chapels were abandoned and sacked, and the ancient monastery became troop headquarters and stables. Some functions of the absent priest were carried on by *rezanderos,* laymen who knew prayers from memory and who charged a fee for saying prayers for the dying, for difficult deliveries, and the like.

By late 1919 the state of Morelos again was peaceful and the village of Tepoztlán began its struggle back to normalcy. When the dispersed villagers returned from the hills and nearby villages they were without homes and in absolute poverty. Loss of life in battle and starvation and illness had again caused a rapid decline in the population; in 1921 there were only 2,156 persons in the village and 3,000 in the municipio.

Post-Revolutionary Period, 1920-40

The Revolution transformed the social structure of Tepoztlán. Some of the *caciques* or their sons returned to their battered or burned homes, but they had lost most of their wealth, particularly their cattle and their shops. It was necessary for all, rich and poor, to begin to build again. But the building took place in a new social framework. The participation by the villagers in the Zapatista forces had left its imprint on the psychology of the people and had acted as a distinct leveling influence. The revolutionary slogans of the Zapatistas had been "land and liberty" and "down with the *caciques.*" Now the political dominance of the *caciques* was gone.

A fundamental economic change had also occurred, and it was one of the most important effects of the Revolution: the communal lands of the municipio (which constitute about 80 percent of all the lands) were again available to the villagers. And in 1929, under the National *Ejido* program, the village received additional lands from a nearby hacienda for distribution to landless families. This further broadened the landbase in the village and helped to increase production.

The political history of the village during the twenty-five years after the Revolution was intense, dramatic, and often tragic. It centered on the issue of the preservation of the forests and other commercial resources. Since the neighboring haciendas had been destroyed and work was scarce, the villagers began cutting down the forests for the commercial production of charcoal. Two groups then arose: one, chiefly ex-Zapatistas, wanted to conserve the forest resources; the other, led by sons of former *caciques,* favored their continued exploitation. These two factions, known as the Bolsheviki (later the Fraternales) and the Centrales, struggled for village control throughout the twenties and thirties, with assassinations, imprisonments, and even massacre marking their conflict. In 1930, a cooperative for producing charcoal was organized. At one time it numbered over five hundred members but by 1937, after many bitter political conflicts, it went into bankruptcy and was dissolved.

Because of its proximity to both state and national capitals, Tepoztlán is particularly subject to outside political influences, and almost every political current of national importance during this period had some repercussions in the village. In 1920, the Colonia Tepozteco, an organization of Tepoztecans living in Mexico City, was founded to eliminate illiteracy and preserve the Nahuatl language in the village. This organization became a major outside political force in the village and a permanent and active urbanizing influence.

The position of the church following the Revolution went through several changes in Tepoztlán. When peace was first restored, the priest returned to the village and religious life was resumed but without its former splendor. The new tranquility was shattered in 1926, however, when the Archbishop of Mexico ordered a policy of noncooperation with the government. All priests were to leave their churches and to cease public religious services. Tepoztlán's priest left the village and only clandestine services by the *rezanderos* were available for a time. Finally, in about 1929, regular church services were again resumed.

In the early thirties, Protestantism came to Tepoztlán when about fifteen families, most of them poor, became Seventh Day Adventists. These families were ostracized, their houses were stoned, and their children were the butt of jokes and abuses. In the face of such hostility their number dwindled. The Catholic church waged successful propaganda campaigns against other Protestant projects, and the villagers came to be suspicious of any strangers who might be non-Catholic.

Two technological innovations which reached Tepoztlán in the 1920's made great changes in the lives of the women. In 1925, the first commercial mill for grinding corn was built, but soon closed because of opposition from the men. In 1927, however, another mill met with financial success through "the revolution of the women against the authority of the men," and by 1942 there were four mills in the village which all the women regularly patronized. From the mills they gained from four to six hours of freedom daily from the grinding stone, and their new leisure enabled them to undertake commercial ventures such as the raising of fruit and animals for marketing. The sewing machine, which made its appearance in the village during this period, also lightened the women's work.

An event of great importance in the history of the village was the completion in 1936 of an asphalt road connecting Tepoztlán with the Mexico City—Cuernavaca highway. This road allowed more frequent and varied social contacts; it brought in the tourist trade; and it gave the village easy access to new markets for its fruits and other produce. Two bus lines were formed, both of them owned and operated as cooperatives by Tepoztecans. The bus lines not only improved means of communication but also became new economic and political factors in the village. The bitter competition between them divided the village into two factions. Their leaders took over political control from the peasants, and the employees constituted the first important group of non-farmers in Tepoztlán.

The school became another important agent of culture change in the village. Enrollment soared from less than 100 in 1926 to 611 in 1944. The school increased literacy, taught the children new standards of personal hygiene and cleanliness, and in effect became a symbol of the new in Tepoztlán.

In the twenty-year post-Revolutionary period, then, there were numerous primary influences for change in the village. The granting of *ejido* lands, the building of corn mills, the new road, and the expansion of school facilities were the most effective of these. The fact that they occurred at about the same time made them mutually reinforcing and the tempo of change was thereby accelerated. The cultural changes that resulted were far reaching: a rapid increase in population, an improvement in health services, a marked rise in the standard of living and the aspiration level of the people, the growth of a class of small landowners, the development of a greater variety and specialization in occupation, a decrease in the use of Nahuatl and a corresponding spread in the use of Spanish, a rise in literacy and the beginning of regular newspaper reading, and a greater incorporation of the village into the mainstream of national life.

Home of an old *cacique*.

3

Economics

THE ECONOMY of Tepoztlán is essentially a household economy of small producers, peasants, artisans, and merchants whose primary motive for production is subsistence. But it is not a self-sufficient economy and probably was not one even in pre-Conquest days. The village depends heavily upon trade with nearby regions for basic elements of diet such as salt, sugar, rice, and chile. From urban centers it obtains cloth, agricultural implements, sewing machines, Coleman lamps, kerosene, guns, patent medicines, water pipes, buses, and pool tables. It has few handicrafts, no pottery, no weaving, and no basketmaking.

From the point of view of agriculture, the basic means of livelihood, the resources of Tepoztlán are poor indeed. Only about 15 percent of the total land area is cultivable by plow and oxen and about 10 percent by the more primitive method of cutting and burning and hoe culture. Even if there were a perfectly equitable distribution of land there would be only 1.5 acres of cultivatable land per capita and about 8 acres of forest and grazing lands per capita. Furthermore, as has been noted, there is no irrigation and only one harvest a year. Since the village cannot support itself by farming alone, Tepoztecans seek other sources of income and are busy at a variety of jobs during different seasons of the year.

The Tepoztecan economy, though that of a peasant society, is neither simple nor primitive. It has many elements: well-developed concepts of private property, a high degree of individualism, a free market, a definition of wealth in terms of land and cattle and other forms of property, a relatively wide range in wealth differences, the use of money, a highly developed system of marketing and trade, interest on capital, work for wages, pawning of property, renting of land, the use of plow and oxen, and specialization in part-time occupations.

Despite this roster of familiar traits, the Tepoztecan economic system is quite distinctive and defies easy classification in terms of such traditional

24

categories as capitalistic or feudal. For side by side with the above traits are others—namely, communal land ownership, collective labor, hoe culture, production primarily for subsistence, barter, the absence of credit institutions, the lack of capital, the fear of displaying wealth except on ceremonial occasions, and the continued importance of religion and ritual in economic pursuits. A further complicating factor is that Tepoztecan economy and technology represent a fusion of elements from three distinct historical levels: the pre-Hispanic, the Spanish-colonial, and the modern western European.

Division of Labor

Division of labor by sex is clearly delineated. Men are expected to support their families by doing most of the work in the fields, by caring for the cattle, horses, oxen, and mules, by making charcoal and cutting wood, and by carrying on all the larger transactions of buying and selling. In addition, most of the specialized occupations—carpentry, masonry, and shoemaking—are filled by men. At home the men provide wood and water, make or repair furniture or work tools, repair the house, and help pick fruit. They also shell corn when the shelling is on a large scale. Politics and local government as well as the organization and management of religious and secular fiestas are also in the hands of the men.

Women's work centers about the care of the family and the house. Women cook, clean, wash, iron, do the daily marketing, shell corn for daily consumption, and care for the children. Mothers train their daughters in women's work and supervise them until their marriage. Many women raise chickens, turkeys, and pigs to supplement the family income; some grow fruit, vegetables, and flowers. Women also buy and sell on a small scale and control the family purse. Tepoztecan women are not expected to work in the fields and they look down on the women of neighboring villages who do so.

In general, women's work is less rigidly defined than men's. Many women, especially widows, engage in men's work without censure. In contrast, men almost never do women's work; the few who do are objects of ridicule. Only in the field, where there are no women, will men build a fire and warm their food without compunction. When a wife is ill or otherwise incapacitated the husband will seek out the assistance of a female relative or, even though poor, hire a servant. Occasionally one hears of a widower or bachelor who cooks and sweeps the house, but never of a man who washes or irons or grinds corn to make tortillas. For a man to be seen carrying corn to the mill is a great humiliation.

Women who have no one to support them may hire themselves out as domestic servants, laundresses, or seamstresses, or may become itinerant peddlers. The only profession an educated woman can practice in the village is that of school teacher. As a rule, women play only a minor part in public activities. The lack of rigidity in the definition of women's occupations, however, is reflected in the fact that on two occasions in the recent past, a woman has held the job of secretary of the local government, a post traditionally filled by men. Women are also members of religious organizations as well as of school committees.

Although 90 percent of the gainfully employed are agriculturists and the occupation of farming has high status, farming is not the sole occupation, as has been indicated, but is combined in various ways with other activities. Some Tepoztecans work on nearby plantations, others engage in trade or raise livestock. In 1948 there were about twenty-six nonagricultural occupations in which a total of 273 individuals took part. The occupations with the largest numbers include storekeepers (20), teachers (21), masons (25), bakers (23), *curanderos* and midwives (28), and rope makers (42). The next largest group consists of butchers (15), barbers (15), corn merchants (13), charcoal makers (13), tile and brickmakers (12), and employees of the bus line (17). In addition, there are shoemakers (5), carpenters (9), ironworkers (3), *chirimiteros*[1] (6), *huehuechiques*[2] (2), firework makers (6), mask makers (6), *mágicos* (1), silver workers (2), millers (3), druggists (2), chauffeurs (6), and plumbers (2). Fifty-three of the 273 individuals engaged in these occupations were women but they were found in only six of the twenty-six occupations, predominantly in teaching and curing.

The twenty-six occupations listed above represent a peculiar mixture of the old and the new. Some, like the *chirimiteros, huehuechiques, curanderos,* masons, mask makers, charcoal makers, and rope makers, probably had their counterpart in pre-Hispanic days. Others, such as storekeepers, shoemakers, and carpenters, have probably existed in the village since the colonial period. Still others—the teachers, bakers, millers, druggists, chauffeurs, and bus employees—are clearly more modern; most of the latter group date from the time of the construction of the road in 1936.

Land Tenure

Three kinds of land tenure are found in Tepoztlán: communal land holdings, *ejido* holdings, and private holdings. Communal lands comprise approximately 80 percent of the land of the municipio and include four of the five land types, *texcal* (see page 31), *monte, cerros,* and *terrenos cerriles.* The communal lands belong traditionally to the municipio and are under its control. They are not divided up into plots.

Ejido lands constitute somewhat less than 5 percent of the land within the municipio and consist primarily of arable land for plow agriculture. *Ejido* lands are communally owned by the municipio but are under the control of locally elected *ejido* authorities rather than the regular municipal authorities. *Ejido* holdings differ from communal holdings in that they are divided into small plots and assigned to individuals in accord with the rules of eligibility

---

[1] Men who play traditional music on the chapel roofs at fiestas in celebration of the saints. They play the *chirimia,* a native flute.

[2] Men who perform traditional ritual in Nahuatl at some of the fiestas.

established by the National *ejido* Program. Title to the *ejido* lands rests with the nation whereas title to the municipal land rests with the municipio.

Ejido and private holdings are practically identical except that while the latter can be bought and sold, the former may remain in the same family for many years and may be passed from father to son if the need for the land can be satisfactorily proved. Private holdings also consist mostly of land used for plow agriculture, and they constitute about 15 percent of the land in the municipio. Private holdings are in fee simple and ownership must be proved by legal title. It is important to remember that in Tepoztlán all three types of land holdings are worked individually rather than collectively.

The communal lands represent one of the oldest forms of landholding, and in Tepoztlán they have shown a remarkable stability down through the years. Actually, the system of communal landholding has remained practically intact through both the Aztec and Spanish conquests. Indeed, the similarity between the policy of the Spanish and of the Aztec conquerors of Tepoztlán toward the system of communal landholdings is noteworthy.

The titles for the communal landholdings of the municipio are precious possessions to the villagers and responsibility for their safekeeping is entrusted to one of the members of the local government in Tepoztlán. These titles are used principally in settling boundary disputes with neighboring municipios. The disputes have been going on for hundreds of years and loss and recovery of the land titles have occurred again and again in the history of the municipio.

In theory, any individual from any one of the eight villages of the municipio has the right to use any of the communal lands in the municipio provided he obtains permission from the municipal authorities or, as at the present time, from the forestry and *ejido* authorities. In practice, however, each of the eight villages has come to consider certain lands, generally those nearest the particular village, as its own. Thus moral boundaries have developed and are recognized by all concerned.

Although the municipio of Tepoztlán has managed to hold most of the communal lands intact against the encroachment of neighboring haciendas, before the Revolution of 1910-20 the *caciques* or ruling elite of the village prohibited the rest of the villagers from using the communal lands in order to assure a cheap labor supply for themselves. One of the most important results of the Revolution was that the communal lands were made available to all Tepoztecans.

The *ejido* lands are a relatively recent phenomenon, dating from after the Revolution. In 1929, Tepoztlán received 2,100 hectares of land in restitution from the Hacienda of Oacalco. Two hundred and sixty-seven (31 percent) Tepoztecan families now hold *ejido* parcels all of which are less than three hectares in size. Of these families, 109 also own private land; the remaining 158 have *ejidos* only.

Only 36 percent or 311 of the 853 families in the village own private land. Thus in a village where the family ideal is to own a plot of land, 64 percent own no land. Moreover, the landholdings are extremely small: over

90 percent of all holdings are less than nine hectares and 68 percent are less than four hectares. A villager with fifteen or more hectares is considered a large landowner, and only two holdings are between twenty-five and twenty-nine hectares. The size of cornfields, incidentally, is very small because many of the holdings are fragmented into parcels which are located in different places. The large number of landless people and the small size of holdings result primarily from the poverty of resources, however, rather than from the concentration of landownership in the hands of a few individuals.

The land problem in Tepoztlán is not a recent one. It was at least as severe in the twenties before the *ejido* grants and it was certainly more acute before the Revolution. Thirty years ago the 158 families who now have *ejido* parcels were landless. Thus the *ejido* program in Tepoztlán has had at least two beneficial effects. It has reduced the number of landless families and it has helped some families who had insufficient land to increase their holdings. But the *ejido* program has by no means solved the land problem, since 384 families still remain landless and have little prospect of becoming landowners. Nor has Tepoztlán benefited from the great advances in agriculture which have occurred in other parts of Mexico as a result of hydroelectric projects and of mechanization. There is still not a single tractor in the village and most families continue to work their tiny subsistence holdings by means of primitive methods.

Agricultural Systems

Two contrasting types of agriculture which represent different historical and technological levels exist side by side in Tepoztlán. One is the primitive pre-Hispanic cutting and burning system of hoe culture; the other is the more modern post-Hispanic agriculture which uses plow and oxen. The differences between hoe culture, locally known as *tlacolol,* and plow culture are not limited to the use of different tools; each system has far-reaching social and economic implications.

In Tepoztlán, both plow culture and hoe culture have been known since the Spanish Conquest. In hoe culture the land used is steep and rocky, while in plow culture it is less sloping, relatively treeless, and includes the broad valley bottom in the southern part of the municipio. Hoe culture is practiced on communally owned land and necessitates a great deal of time and labor but very little capital. Plow culture is practiced on privately owned land and requires relatively little time and labor but considerable capital. The former depends almost exclusively on family labor; the latter depends to a greater extent on hired labor. In hoe culture the yields are much larger than in plow culture, but the amount of corn planted by each family is relatively small and never reaches the amount planted by a few of the larger operators in plow culture. In hoe culture rotation of land is a necessity, for the fields cease to produce after the first few years; in plow culture the same fields may be planted year after year until the soil is completely exhausted.

Hoe culture is essentially geared to production for subsistence, while plow culture is better geared to production for the market. It is significant that most families who work *tlacolol* are landless and that *tlacolol* has traditionally been viewed as the last resort of the poor. Farmers who own small plots of land, however, may also work some *tlacolol* to supplement their meager income. Indeed, in the past few years inflation has brought a new trend to the village. Tepoztecans who own considerable land now rent it out or let it rest and work *tlacolol*. Twelve of twenty families who own private land and also hold an *ejido* grant now work *tlacolol;* these twelve are among the large landowners. This is resented by most *tlacololeros* who believe that the communal lands should serve the landless.

Other differences between hoe culture and plow culture include the cycles of work, the tools, the type of corn, the work techniques, and even the terminology. Generally speaking, the tools and techniques used in *tlacolol* are still known by their Nahuatl names, while in plow culture Spanish names prevail. Still another difference results from the location of the lands involved. With few exceptions the privately owned land used for plow culture is much closer to the village than the *tlacolol* lands. *Tlacololeros* usually rise at 4:00 A.M., walk for about two or three hours to reach their fields, and return home a few hours later than plow culture farmers.

The basic tools of production in plow culture are the plow, the machete, and the hoe and ax. Two types of plow are used: the *arado criollo* (wooden plow) and the *arado polco* (steel plow). The wooden plow was introduced by the Spaniards shortly after the Conquest. Before the Revolution of 1910-20 the steel plow was used only by a small number of families, and as late as 1926-27 Redfield reported only a few steel plows. By the early thirties, however, plows generally became more widely used, and in 1943 most farmers had steel plows as well as wooden plows, each kind being used for different operations. In 1943, approximately 213 families in the village (or 48 percent) owned plows.

Oxen have been used in the village since colonial times. In 1944, however, there were only 179 teams of oxen and only 57 percent of the landowners had oxen. There is little local buying and selling of oxen; most of them are bought in the neighboring state of Guerrero, although for many years the trip there was dangerous. The few villagers who traveled to Guerrero did so with considerable risk but also with considerable profit.

The work cycle of plow culture consists of four stages; preparing the land, planting, cultivating, and harvesting. The breaking of new land is known as the *barbecho;* the plowing of land formerly under cultivation is known as *los tres arados*. The system of plowing used in each case differs considerably. Most farmers prefer to break new land during the rainy season, generally in August, in preparation for planting the following year. The steel plow is used in the *barbecho* and the land is plowed in one continuous furrow to form a concentric rectangle. Tepoztecans pride themselves on having straight rows of corn and compete with one another to see who can plow the straightest.

One man with a single team of oxen can plow on an average of about two-fifths of an acre a day. If time permits, about two *barbechos* are made. In preparing a field that was under cultivation the previous year, the steel plow also is used and three plowings are made. The third plowing forms part of the process of planting.

Planting usually starts in early June after the rains have begun. The selection of seed for planting is generally made soon after the harvest in January; at that time the finest ears of corn are set aside to be shelled in May or June just before planting. Some Tepoztecans still hold to the tradition of having the seed blessed by the priest on May 15th, the day of San Isidro. The women select about ten of the finest ears of corn as well as some of the best beans and squash and take them to the church. They may also take along some copal and a censer. As they burn incense in the church the priest appears and blesses the seed with holy water. The corn that has been blessed is placed in the corn fields to rot; it must not be burned or the seed will not grow.

The ancient custom of addressing the seed in Nahuatl is no longer practiced but is still remembered by most men over fifty. The corn was spoken to in a short formal ritual just before it was planted in the fields, and often this ceremony was the occasion of great emotion and even of weeping. One of the speeches began, "My beloved body and strength go and bear the cold and the storm of the seasons; all is for us." A few Tepoztecans still follow a similar ritual today except that the recitations are in Spanish and the references are to the Christian God. "God bless you. I bury you and if you return while I live the satisfaction will be mine; if not then my descendants."

The corn fields usually are cultivated two or three times at twenty-day intervals. After the third cultivation, about mid-August, the corn plants in the first and last two rows of the *milpa* are hilled by hand with the *coa*. This hilling symbolizes the end of cultivation and it is looked upon as a decoration or an adornment of the work of cultivation. It also serves to strengthen the outside rows against the wind and Tepoztecans believe that it protects inside of the corn field.

The termination of cultivation is celebrated by a fiesta both in the fields and at home. Immediately after the last hilling some of the villagers walk around the field and recite the following typical speech: "Now I have fulfilled my obligations of attending and cultivating you as you deserve. Now if you do not want to produce, that is your responsibility. For my part I now retire." A wooden cross is sometimes put in the center of the *milpa* after the last row is cultivated, and prayers and religious songs are intoned by the owner. Fireworks are set off, and bread and cheese, tequila and punch are served to the workers. The oxen are decorated with flowers and with pictures of San Isidro. The oxen are then driven home, more food and drink are consumed, and firecrackers are set off in the patio.

Toward the end of September when the first corn is ripe, the villagers go to the fields for another celebration during which they roast corn and drink punch. On September 28th, the day of San Miguel, they carry crosses made of *pericón* which have been blessed by the priest and place them on each side of the *milpa* to protect it against strong winds. According to an old belief, if the corn is damaged by winds it is because the dancers who represent El Tepozteco at the fiesta of September 8th did not perform properly. Between late September and early November there is little work in the fields. During this time the villagers pick the hog plums from the native *ciruela* trees, look after their animals, cut wood, and take care of various tasks around the house.

Harvesting consists of stripping the leaves in early November and of picking the corn in early December. Each family, sometimes with the aid of hired labor, harvests its own fields. By early January most fields are harvested and the corn is stored in storage bins, usually without being shelled so that it will better resist the corn worms which are a great problem to Tepoztecans. Many families leave the corn on the cob until April or May, the women shelling only what they need for daily use or for small-scale trade. Later the men do large-scale shelling, using as a sheller either the black volcanic rock or dry corncobs bound together in the form of a flat disc over which the corn is rubbed. The shelled corn is usually stored in sacks, although a few families still have the ancient clay storage bin or *cuescomatl.* Many families place a skeleton of a dog's head or a piece of pine wood and lime in the sacks to protect the corn against spoilage. According to an old belief, a death in a house will make the corn more subject to the ravages of insects.

Corn yields vary a great deal from field to field and from year to year on the same field. According to Tepoztcán classifications, first-class land will produce on an average of two *cargas* of corn on the cob for every *cuartillo* of corn seed planted; second-class land will produce an average of one *carga* for each *cuartillo* of seed; third-class land about half a *carga.* Thus the productivity of the best land is about four times that of the poorest. Most Tepoztecans do not use fertilizer; they are aware of its benefits but are unable to use it because of the shortage of manure and the cost of commercial fertilizer.

There is considerable variation in the number of man days of work necessary for clearing, planting, cultivating, and harvesting a corn field. The most important variables are the nature of the terrain, the quality of the soil, the speed of the oxen and the workers, and the type of seed used. The total number of man days of work needed for the production of one hectare of corn ranges from 35 to 65 with about 50 days as an overall average. This estimate, however, does not include the many days the peasant spends in guarding his field against cattle and trespassers. Of the 50 days, by far the most time is spent in cultivation and in harvesting. The preparation of the fields and the planting take relatively little time.

The land used for hoe culture is of two distinct types and located in different parts of the municipio. The first type is known as *texcal,* land covered with black volcanic rock and a semideciduous scrub forest where the leaves fall and rot during the dry season and make a rich but thin topsoil in little pockets among the rocks. The second type is known as *cerros*[3] and refers

---

[3] The term *cerros* here refers both to the spectacular buttelike rock outcroppings which surround the village and to the steep slopes covered with scrub forest.

to the steep slopes or mountainsides. Most of the *cerros* used for hoe culture are lime rockbeds with rock outcroppings. Both types of land are at some distance from the village.

In 1944, there were 189 families, or 21 percent of all families in the village, in which one or more members worked *tlacolol* land. Over 50 percent of these *tlacololeros* lived in the three larger barrios of Tepoztlán but they were only a very small percentage of the total number of families in these barrios. In the smaller and poorer barrios, on the other hand, *tlacololeros* constituted a much higher percentage of the families. About 96 families, or 50 percent, of all *tlacololeros* depended solely upon *tlacolol;* that is they had no private land or *ejido*. Thirty-nine *tlacololeros* owned small private parcels, 34 held *ejidos,* and 20 had both private land and *ejido*.

Most *tlacolol* clearings are small, requiring on the average between eight and twelve *cuartillos* of seed; the largest takes thirty-five. The great amount of labor necessary for clearing *tlacolol* land and the shortage of land are the two main factors responsible for the small size of *tlacolol* plots. Moreover, since *tlacolol* is definitely viewed as subsistence agriculture, any man who cleared inordinately large areas would incur the wrath of other villagers.

The use of plow and oxen for *tlacolol* is ruled out because of the steep and rocky terrain. Work in *tlacolol* begins in January, and a villager requires approximately 50 days to clear enough land to plant twelve *cuartillos* of corn seed. The trees are cut with an ax and the bush is cleared with a machete. Most *tlacolol* clearings are used two years in succession, however. The cut trees and brush dry out until April when they are burned and the ashes used as fertilizer. Enclosures of rocks and brush are built around the clearings to keep out stray animals. Planting begins in May before the rains. A small hole about four to six inches deep is made wherever there is enough soil, and the seeds are dropped in. There are no orderly rows and, unlike plow culture methods, there is no cultivation. There is usually only one weeding, after which the corn is left to grow, but occasional visits are made to the clearings to check the enclosures. Harvest procedures are very much the same as for plow culture.

One of the most striking differences between hoe and plow culture is the much greater amount of time necessary for the former. Approximately three times more man days are needed to produce one hectare of corn in *tlacolol* than in plow culture—that is, an average of 150 days as compared to 50. The single job of weeding by hand takes more time than all three cultivations with plow. There is also a great difference in the total time spent in preparation of the land, and a somewhat longer time period is spent for harvesting and transporting in *tlacolol* than in plow culture because the *tlacolol* fields are farther from the village. Fencing the *tlacolol* is time consuming and must be repeated each time a new *tlacolol* is opened; private *milpas* and *ejidos* in contrast have permanent stone fences.

In addition to the difference in actual time spent, there is also a difference in the nature of the work. Work in *tlacolol* is infinitely more exhausting than work in plow culture. Weeding by hand leaves welts on the hands of the toughest *tlacololero* that last for days and it is said that a *tlacololero* is known by his hands. But there is less time pressure in *tlacolol*. A man can clear his land any time between January and April. He can work for a few days at a clearing, spend a few days doing some other job, then return to the clearing. After planting there is considerable time leeway before the first and only weeding. This is not the case in plow culture, where once a field has been planted the cultivations must follow at regular intervals or the yield will be appreciably cut. The differences between the work cycles of the two systems are shown in the following chart:

Plow Culture	*Month*	*Hoe Culture*
	January	Clearing land with
	February	machete and ax
No work in fields	March	No work
	April	Burning brush,
	May	fencing, seeding
Clearing land, plowing, seeding	June	
First cultivation	July	Reseeding
Second cultivation		
Third cultivation	August	Weeding
Visits to field	September	
Weeding	October	Visits to field
Stripping corn stalks	November	
Harvesting and transporting corn	December	Harvesting and transporting corn

The average yield from hoe culture is about twice as high as that from plow culture. This would seem to make hoe culture very attractive, but there are a number of reasons why more villagers do not work *tlacolol*. The difficulty of the work discourages many, and the fact that *tlacolol* has traditionally been considered work for the poor and for the Indian is also a factor. Furthermore, many families who work as peons have no corn at harvest and must earn cash to support themselves. In other words, even in the case of *tlacolol* which takes so little capital, a man must have some corn (capital) to tide him over the long periods of time necessary for clearing the scrub forest. By far the most important reason, however, is the limited amount of *tlacolol* land, a shortage which has been felt more and more as the number of *tlacololeros* has increased. By its very nature the *tlacolol* system of cutting and burning demands large reserve areas, for it takes about ten years for cleared land to grow back into scrub forest and be worth clearing again. If all the villagers were to open *tlacolol* clearings in a single year, plantings in new clearings could not be made again for at least ten years.

At the base of this situation is one of the crucial problems in Tepoztlán —namely, the rapid increase of population with no accompanying increase in resources or improvement in the techniques of production. The increase in the number of *tlacololeros* represents rather a return to a more primitive type of production in an effort to escape the devastating effects of a money economy during a period of inflation. *Tlacolol* helps to resolve the immediate problem but it is by no means a satisfactory long-range solution. Were Tepoztlán a primitive culture with a small population, the system of *tlacolol,* although wasteful and inefficient, might be feasible. But in the face of an increasing population and of higher standards of living, the primitive *tlacolol* no longer is adequate. The necessity of clearing new plots of land every second or third year, the rapid depletion of the land and its forest resources, and the consequent danger of erosion are problems which will soon have to be reckoned with.

Livestock, Industry, and Trade

Tepoztlán has relatively little livestock and most of it is of poor quality. The Revolution of 1910-20 destroyed most of the herds and the present supply has been acquired slowly and with difficulty since that time. Cattle raising has never been an important industry in Tepoztlán and was never well integrated into the local economy. Climate and topographical conditions in the municipio are not conducive to large-scale stock raising, since the land is steep, rocky, and forested and the little level land is used for agriculture. Beginning in December, pasture becomes progressively scarcer and by March the cattle are excessively thin. During these months the herds are generally reduced by 15 to 20 percent.

The care given to animals is minimal and consists mostly of guarding them against being stolen or lost. Much time is devoted to this, irrespective of whether a family owns one or two animals or a herd of thirty or forty, for cattle stealing is one of the major hazards of cattle raising. Some families have lost over twenty-five head of cattle in a few years. It is said that cattle stealing increases markedly before important fiestas. Cattle owners often pay the priest to say a Mass for the protection of the cattle.

Animal ownership is on a small scale and is limited to a relatively small proportion of the villagers. Only 179, or 21 percent, of the families own cattle. Well over 50 percent of these families have between one and three cows and about 40 percent from four to ten cows. In 1943, the largest herd was over seventy head although estimates obtained in 1947 showed two herds of 150 head each. Cattle owners are expected to contribute generously to religious fiestas. When a villager sells a cow or an ox he usually lights a candle to El Señor de Ixcatepec. At rodeos and bullfights the larger herdowners contribute bulls and also money for *ponche* and fireworks. Most cattle owners have an image of San Antonio, the patron saint of cattle, in their homes. To keep cattle from wandering away it is customary to cut off hair from the ear of the cow or ox and bury it under the hearth.

The ownership of oxen is limited to 177, or 20 percent, of the families. This low percentage indicates the small extent to which Tepoztecan peasants own one of the basic means of production. The distribution of horses, donkeys, and mules as owned by families—28 percent, 11 percent, and 14 percent, respectively—reflects the local evaluation of work animals. Mules are more popular than donkeys, and horses are valued most highly. Riding horses in contrast to work horses are considered a luxury. The prestige associated with horse ownership probably goes back to the colonial period when only the leading men in the village were allowed to ride horses. Hogs are more generally owned by the villagers: about 40 percent of Tepoztecan families have at least one hog and many have two or three.

Most of the animals that are used for food are slaughtered in the village itself, for there is very little trade in cattle or hogs outside of the municipio. There is also relatively little buying and selling of cattle and oxen within the village since most of these animals are traditionally purchased in the state of Guerrero where prices are lower. The price of livestock, like that of most items, has increased sharply since the turn of the century, but the sharpest increase has occurred since 1940.

Milk is sold locally by about a dozen families, the local market consisting of a small but growing group of school teachers and Mexican tourists. Most of the milk produced, however, is converted into cheese which also is sold in the village. Milk products are used for medicinal purposes—whey, cheese, and butter for skin rashes and cheese as a poultice for snake bites. Some families use as a purgative milk in which a cow's tail has been soaked.

The production of charcoal is one of the most important sources of income for many families, especially for the poor. Generally it is carried on as a part-time activity by farmers during the slack season, but in the smaller barrios of San Sebastian, San Pedro, and Los Reyes it is a full-time occupation for many men. Until 1947, most of the charcoal was transported by burro to Yautepec, but since that time the bus line has agreed to transport it and now much of it goes to Cuernavaca.

Another important supplementary source of income for farmers is the sale of *ciruelas* or hog plums. Although they first became a cash crop when the railroad was built, it was not until the building of the highway in the thirties that trade in plums expanded. Merchants from Mexico City and Cuernavaca now send their trucks to Tepoztlán during the harvest to gather up the fruit which has been brought together by a few Tepoztecan middlemen.

Rope making is an important home industry among the poorer families in the barrio of San Sebastian. It is a family affair, requiring two or three persons for the major operation of twisting. The *ixtle* fiber is obtained from the maguey plants which grow on the communal lands. Only about a half of the persons who make rope gather their own *ixtle* fiber, however; the other half buy it.

Circulation and Distribution of Goods

Circulation of goods in the municipio is carried on by means of the local market, stores, itinerant merchants, intervillage trade, the sale and purchase of goods in Cuernavaca and other large towns, and the exchange and barter of goods between families in the village. Changes in the means of communication during the last twenty years have made some of these factors more important than others. In general, the effect of the highway has been to weaken the local market, to increase the importance of stores and trade relations with Cuernavaca, to decrease the extent of intervillage trade within the municipio, and to abolish completely earlier trade relations with other villages in the region.

The market days in Tepoztlán are Wednesdays and Sundays. As in Redfield's time, vendors from the satellite villages and from more distant localities gather in the central plaza where they offer their wares. Each of the seven villages of the municipio has its traditional place in the market, but it is only on a rare occasion that vendors from all the villages appear on the same day. In comparison with intervillage markets in a Oaxaca town of comparable size, the Tepoztecan market seems very poor indeed. Relatively little care is given to the display of food, and goods are limited in variety.

No organized credit facilities exist in Tepoztlán, nor is there any *ejido* credit. A few money lenders make loans at an interest rate of from 10 to 12 percent per month. Money loans are made by oral or written agreement but in many cases some property is necessary as security. The practice of pawning property as security for a loan is common. Usually the property is land, oxen, or *ciruela* trees, but smaller items such as an iron or even a woman's *rebozo* may be pawned for small loans from neighbors. Borrowing money is for the most part limited to emergency situations—for food, doctors, medicine, a funeral, or a wedding. There is little borrowing for investment in capital goods or for starting a business. Borrowing is considered more as an act of desperation than as a matter of everyday business. The idea of borrowing money from the bank in Cuernavaca is foreign to the thinking of all but a few sophisticated villagers.

Wealth Differences

The concepts of rich and of poor are frequently used by the villagers, but the terms are used in a relative way, are not easily defined, and are applied as a rule to individuls rather than to groups. All Tepoztecans tend to characterize themselves as poor, and there is little ostentatious display of wealth on the part of the rich. As noted earlier, the concealing of wealth is a deep-seated trait, the purpose of concealment being to avoid envy, the claims of friends, and taxes and contributions to the church and public affairs. Such an attitude tends to limit the function of wealth as a factor in social stratification. This is not to say, however, that there is a cult of poverty or that poverty is considered a desirable state.

In general, the rich are not readily distinguishable from the poor. Both work the land dressed in the same white *calzones* and huaraches; both hire day laborers when necessary. Men who own property, as well as those who do not, hire themselves out as day laborers when they need cash. Employees are frequently relatives, *compadres,* or friends with whom the employer has a reciprocal arrangement of aid or labor. There are no Tepoztecans who employ workers on a large scale; three or four peons are considered a good number, and they are hired for short periods during the busiest parts of the agricultural cycle. The relations between employer and employee are largely characterized by a spirit of mutual cooperation as well as by a recognition of equality of status. The employer works side by side with his workers, addressing them as *tu* if they are his own age and with the respectful *Usted* if they are older. In most cases a peon works for someone else only if he receives good treatment; frequently he feels that he is conferring a favor upon his employer by working for him. Full-time domestic servants in Tepoztlán are few, for women consider it humiliating to be servants. Orphans or daughters of the very poorest families seek such employment but they prefer to work in Cuernavaca or in Mexico City rather than in their own village.

The village does not have a leisure class nor is there any social stigma attached to physical labor. Many of the rich families were once poor and they cling to the habits of hard work and frugality. A rich man may explain the poverty of a neighbor in terms of his being backward, lazy, and ignorant, but he will treat him with due respect in most situations. There is sensitivity to differences in economic status but there are few barriers to social interaction. The villagers, however, tend to prefer the company of their equals or inferiors to that of people in a superior economic position.

Despite these leveling characteristics, the differences in wealth are striking. The rich have a somewhat higher standard of living than the poor: they eat better, dress better, and live in more comfortable homes. Twelve items were mentioned most frequently by informants as constituting wealth in the village. These were *ejido* plots, privately owned land, teams of oxen, plows, cattle, burros, mules, horses, hogs, sewing machines, plum trees, and urban property—that is, the ownership of more than one housesite. These items all have one characteristic in common: they are all means of production and a source of income.

To rank the families according to their wealth, we devised a point scale using one point for every hundred pesos of value. Points were assigned to each of the above twelve items in accordance with its approximate sale value, its approximate production value, or both. A score was obtained for a given family by adding the number of points accorded to each item. Families were then classified into different groups. It was found that 81 percent fell into the lowest group (point score 0-39); 13.9 percent fell into the middle group (40-99); and 4.4 percent in the upper group (100-407.4). The lowest group may be further broken down into three sub-groups: those with a 0 score, those from 1-19, and those from 20-39; these we shall call I-A, I-B, and I-C respectively. The middle group will be referred to as II, and the upper group as III-A (100-159) and III-B (160 and over).

The families with zero scores consist for the most part of young married men, most of whom live with parents who also have low scores; or they are widows or old men many of whom live alone. One-third of the group consists of women who manage to earn a living by small-scale trade and odd jobs. Groups I-A and I-B, in which there are 511 families with scores of 0-19, contain 97 percent of the landless people of the village and 354, or 70 percent, of the families in this group have zero scores for land. Approximately one-third of these people are *tlacololeros* but all of them depend upon a variety of activities which together with *tlacolol* provide a meager income. Many burn charcoal, sell wood, work as peons, are small traders, or have some other part-time occupation. They have some measure of security in that most of them own their own housesites or will inherit them. About one-third have hogs. Less than a third own a mule, horse, or donkey.

The 119 families in Group II include most of the artisans and merchants as well as the better-to-do farmers. The artisans and merchants are the most acculturated group in the village. They wear ready-made clothing, send their children out of the village to high school, and generally have a higher standard of living.

Group III consists of 38 families all of which have high scores on land, cattle, or both. About one-half of these families inherited their land from wealthy relatives who before the Revolution were *caciques* and dominated the village. The other half have worked their way up to their present position. It is the members of Group III who do not go in for modern dress or for ostentatious spending. They are a hard-working people and not a leisure class. One of their distinguishing characteristics is that they generally have hired men all year around, but they nevertheless work side by side with their peons.

Institutionalized barriers to vertical mobility do not exist in Tepoztlán. No single group has a monopoly of the means of production or of the sources of wealth. Nor does any group control sufficient capital or labor to achieve wealth by its use or exploitation. The rate of capital accumulation is very slow because of the limited natural resources, the poor technology, the low productivity, and also because of the spending patterns, particularly for fiestas. Nevertheless a trend toward the concentration of wealth is apparent, especially in land. The upper economic group, although constituting only 4 percent of all the families, owns approximately 25 percent of the land and this includes some of the best land. Cattle ownership shows a similar trend.

Two points should be emphasized here: first, that there are no younger men as heads of families in the upper economic group; and second, that the majority of the young men now in Group I and II have little prospect of ever achieving a top position. In this sense little upward mobility is possible in Tepoztlán. Most Tepoztecans are themselves convinced of the impossibility of becoming wealthy and accordingly do not organize their lives around the goal of wealth. It is mainly among the families of Group II that higher aspirations obtain and it is in this group that there is some upward mobility.

Despite the wealth differences in Tepoztlán, there are no clearly delineated class differences in the sense of broad social groupings differentiated from each other by distinctive modes of life and cultural expression. Sex, age, kinship, and occupation are the basic factors in social differentiation; differences in wealth, education, and living standards distinguish individuals but not cohesive social groups. As indicated earlier, the economic and social bases for class stratification were largely swept away by the Mexican Revolution of 1910-20. As of 1943, Tepoztlán might best be described as a community with incipient social stratification which will probably become intensified with the greater contacts with the outside, the increased wealth, and greater occupational specialization.

Tepoztlán does not show the full spectrum of the national Mexican class structure. There is no upper class of industrialists, bankers, factory owners, or even large landowners. Nor is there a rural proletariat, since the communal lands are available to the landless. Most of the people, then, are poor peasants and might be classified as a part of the rural lower class segment of Mexico. From a social and economic point of view, the contrast between the landholders and the landless among the peasants is not sharp because most holdings are tiny and Tepoztecans with an acre of land do not live much better than those without it, even though landownership of any size is considered highly desirable. The landless and the landowners certainly do not constitute distinct social classes. Moreover, there is a general similarity in the value systems between most of the people in the nonagricultural occupations and the peasants. In 1943, most of the carpenters, bakers, barbers, mask makers, and merchants were also part-time peasants and almost all of them came from families who were still peasants or of peasant origin.

Carrying corn to the mill.

4

Social Structure

THE SOCIAL STRUCTURE of Tepoztlán may perhaps be best understood in terms of various levels of organization: first, the village as an entity in itself with such village-wide institutions as the school, the church, the market, and so on; second, the village in relation to units smaller than itself and contained within it—namely, the barrio and the family; and third, the village in relation to units larger than itself and of which it is a part— namely, the municipio, the region and state, and the nation. These internal and external aspects of village life are closely interrelated and together constitute a continuum of socioeconomic organization. However, from the point of view of the villagers, the municipio is the crucial dividing line among the various levels. As the villager moves from the nuclear family to the barrio, to the village, and to the municipio, his relationships progressively become somewhat more distant and formal but he is still within a primary community where social, economic, political, and even personal bonds are quite strong. When he moves outside of the municipio of Tepoztlán, however, he moves into another kind of world. Here his knowledge of geography becomes vague, while the distinctions between villager and city person, between *paisano* and stranger, between *gente humilde* and *gente de cultura*, become sharp.

Throughout the levels of social organization certain basic themes or principles may be discerned. One is a strong in-group feeling among the members of a unit (family, barrio, and so forth) in relation to other units at the same level. Barrio members identify with their own barrio against other barrios, with their village against other villages, each jealously guarding its rights. This first principle may be called the isolating or boundary-establishing principle. A certain amount of pride and even of competitiveness is involved here. The in-group feeling should be conceived of as a gradient, however, which is strongest at the family level and becomes weaker as one moves out to the larger units. The occasions for acting out the sense of solidarity occur much less frequently in the larger than in the smaller units. For example, the sense of municipal solidarity will come into play during boundary disputes but a sense of family solidarity might be aroused daily.

A second principle, which runs in a somewhat different if not opposite direction to that of the first, is the principle of nucleation. A related principle is the dominance of the center over the periphery, the larger units over the smaller. The settlement pattern in highland Mexico is characterized by relatively self-contained nuclear groupings or pockets; the small number of villages which make up these pockets are centrally located so that the density of the population decreases almost to zero as one moves from the center to the periphery. Thus the village of Tepoztlán as a central village is dominant over the surrounding villages politically, economically, and socially. Tepoztecans feel superior to the people of the outlying villages and by and large have better means of communication, a higher standard of living, and better educational facilities. As one goes from Tepoztlán to the smaller surrounding villages one finds a greater persistence of older customs, less literacy, and more people who speak the Indian language. A similar relationship may be seen within the village itself between the larger central barrios and the smaller outlying barrios. . .

A third characteristic of the social organization of the village may be termed the principle of familism, by which is meant that an individual's primary loyalties are to his nuclear family. The bonds of kinship are those in which Tepoztecans place the greatest trust, and whatever social relations they have outside of the family are always fraught with caution if not suspicion. This great absorption within the nuclear family, combined with the weakness of the extended family, tends to make for narrow horizons, for self-interest, and for an atomistic quality in the social structure. It also helps to explain much of the quality of interpersonal relations, which will be discussed later. Although the discrete family units are organized into such larger units as the barrio, the village, and the municipio, these organizational forms are relatively impersonal; they do not impinge as directly upon the lives of the individual as does, for example, the extended family, the clan, or the caste, on the members of societies organized on these bases. In addition, the connection between the village and the state and federal government is in terms of elected officials who vote as members of their *demarcación,* an arbitrary political subdivision of the village that has little meaning for the villagers. In other words, in Tepoztlán, unlike more primitive societies, most of the organized relations outside of the immediate family are based upon social, religious, or political factors rather than upon kinship ties.

The nuclear familism of Tepoztlán must be understood from a historical point of view. It may be seen as a defensive reaction to the disorganizing effects of the Spanish Conquest which destroyed the ancient Indian *calpulli* or clan and transferred its landholding and other functions to the newly established village government. Because communal lands have persisted and because most Tepoztecans have not had private landholdings, the extended family has had little opportunity to develop as a corporate landholding group. This explains in part why Tepoztecans have a weak genealogical sense and why, in spite of the stability of the population and the great age of the village, most of them do not know who their great grandparents were. The present-time orientation of the villagers is due in large part to the cutting off of the extended family horizons.

The contemporary social structure of Tepoztlán may be seen as an interaction between two opposing elements, one the more collectivistic tradition of the Indian heritage with its communal lands and collective labor, the other the more individualistic and isolating familism. As we shall see, however, a major trend reveals that both the pre-Hispanic forms and the defensive familism are being superseded by new forms resulting from the increasing integration of the village in the modern Mexican nation.

The Village and the Nation

Three aspects of the relationship between the village and the nation may be distinguished—namely, the villagers' knowledge of the geography and history of the nation, the extent to which they perceive themselves as Mexicans, and the degree to which national institutions operate on the village level and affect the villagers' lives. The villagers think of themselves first and foremost as Tepoztecans but they readily identify themselves as Mexicans. Indeed, they refer to their ancient indigenous language not as Nahuatl but as Mexicano.

Despite this easy linguistic identification, however, their concepts of modern Mexico as a nation are quite limited. Most Tepoztecans know the names of some of the states even though, as of 1948, few had traveled beyond the state of Morelos and portions of the neighboring states of Mexico, Guerrero, and Puebla. But many villagers have had occasion to deal with people from other states. During the Revolution they came into contact with soldiers from various parts of the country; at one time *norteños* from Coahuila camped in Tepoztlán for months, and the villagers still speak of their strange customs. Tepoztecans also are familiar with many of the Mexican regional stereotypes. For example, they "know" that people from Monterrey are stingy and that Yucatecans are squareheads. The geographic horizons of younger people who have had some schooling are, of course, much broader.

The school has been one of the most important agencies in developing an awareness of and a sense of identification with the nation. With the federalization of the schools in the twenties, texts and teaching materials were standardized. The Mexican government eliminated most texts written by foreigners and substituted those written by Mexicans. The latter, seeking to arouse Mexican nationalism, used stories of Mexican Indians rather than of children of other lands and gave Mexican national heroes a prominent place. Moreover, the school personnel in Tepoztlán began to be recruited from various parts of the country rather than, as formerly, only from Morelos. Tepoztecans have had teachers from Yucatan, Oaxaca, Jalisco, and Nuevo Leon, and from them they have learned about the dances and customs of other regions.

The large new elementary school building, named *Escuadrón 201* after a squadron of Mexican aviators who were stationed in the Philippines in World War II, stands as a symbol of *Mexicanidad* to the villagers. The school was constructed in the early forties with national funds on the direct order of President Avila Comacho. Thanks to the school, the commemoration of such national holidays as September 15 (national independence) is assuming more importance in the village. At these times parents outfit their children in new uniforms, at a great sacrifice, and local officials prepare for the event months in advance.

Paralleling the work of the school is that of the traveling cultural mission, also a federal service, which has been visiting Tepoztlán for a number of years. The mission taught Tepoztecans how to make beds, chairs, and other furniture; it taught the girls sewing, knitting, and crocheting; it encouraged social dancing and sports like volleyball; it taught some women how to make inexpensive preserves; and it worked toward improving homes by persuading a few families to build privies (now in disuse) and to raise the hearth off the floor for more sanitary cooking. A mission doctor administered injections and gave advice on baby care.

Another federal service, the campaign against illiteracy, also reached Tepoztlán and helped somewhat to develop a greater awareness of the Mexican nation. Slogans used included "Mexico must be great because of its culture" and "The Fatherland must have citizens who can read." Publications which occasionally reach Tepoztlán are leaflets put out by the official party, presidential messages, and propaganda leaflets from some of the larger labor unions. The reading public in the village is still very small, however.

Other federal agencies which directly or indirectly influence the daily lives of Tepoztecans include the Department of Health, the Department of Agriculture, the Department of Indian Affairs, the Department of National Economy, *Gobernación,* and the Federal Supreme Court. All of these agencies have files on the village which date from the twenties and which reflect their increasing role in village life. Federal taxation, which touches most Tepoztecans directly, is a common subject of complaint even though the villagers pay relatively few taxes; these are mainly on the sale of charcoal, the slaughter of animals, and trade. The federal government has maintained a health clinic in Cuernavaca for years but the Tepoztecans still prefer *curanderos.* The Agrarian Department intervenes directly in the affairs of those Tepoztecans who hold land under the *ejido* program. The nationalization of some of the communal lands has lessened local control and has caused some resentment on the part of the villagers. National control of forest resources also has not gained the approval of Tepoztecans, especially when it conflicts with their local interests as in the case of charcoal production.

Perhaps the Tepoztecan peasant sees the power of the federal government most clearly in the form of federal troops. Tepoztecans are suspicious of and dislike soldiers, and when military conscription was first instituted in the forties they tried to resist it. Local feeling against conscription reached its climax when it was rumored by the Sinarquists (a right-wing political group that sympathized with the Nazis) that the young men were being prepared to fight against the Germans on orders given by the United States.

The Mexican Revolution was one of the most important factors in developing a sense of nationalism among Tepoztecans. Many of them joined the ranks of the Zapatistas and traveled widely with the guerrilla forces. Some of the *caudillos* of the Revolution, such as Zapata and Obregón, established the custom of visiting the peasants personally and discussing their problems. General Lázaro Cárdenas continued the practice, and the villagers remember his visit to Tepoztlán with pride. In 1935, Cárdenas arrived on foot without previous announcement or preparation. He set up a temporary office in the atrium of the church, where the Tepoztecans could come to see him. Their chief request was for help with the construction of the road to Cuernavaca. When their request was granted and the road was built with federal help, they began to think of the president not only as a representative of a powerful government but also as a popular figure and a friend of the peasants. It is now not uncommon for Tepoztecans to send requests or protests directly to the president. Indeed this has happened in almost every case of conflict between village factions or of boundary quarrels with neighboring municipios.

The national elections for president which occur every six years also give Tepoztecans contact with political affairs of nation-wide scope. Before the elections, delegates and politicians come to the village to organize local committees for the support of a particular group or candidate. During the campaigns the villagers begin to realize that they are acting not only as Tepoztecans but also as citizens of the Mexican nation.

Some indication of the Tepoztecan sense of belonging to the nation may be gathered from their reaction to the question of Mexico's participation in World War II. Most Tepoztecans were opposed to Mexican entrance into the war on the side of the democracies. Under the influence of Sinarquist propaganda, sympathy with the Axis powers first developed among a small but vocal sector of the population. Rumors began to circulate that Zapata was not really dead but was fighting with Hitler; this was why the Germans were winning so many victories. Latent anti-U.S. sentiment was fanned by further rumors that the Mexicans were being asked to fight to save the "gringos." The Tepoztecans accepted the Mexican declaration of war against the Axis as one of those decisions of an omnipotent federal government about which nothing could be done.

Just as Tepoztecans recognize an administrative hierarchy whose seat is in Mexico City so they recognize a religious hierarchy headed by the archbishop in Mexico City. The church in Tepoztlán has taken part in most of the recent campaigns of the national and international church organization to strengthen the church. For example, when the four hundredth anniversary of the Virgin of Guadalupe was celebrated throughout Mexico, church dignitaries came to the village to explain the great miracle of the apparition of the Virgin to Juan Diego shortly after the Conquest.

The Village and the State of Morelos

The average Tepoztecan has a more precise notion of the geography of the state of Morelos than of the nation. During the years of the Revolution many Tepoztecans traveled over large portions of the state, and many have taken trips for economic purposes or have made religious pilgrimages. Work on sugar plantations has given others some familiarity with the southern part of the state. The proximity of the state capital, Cuernavaca, also has played a part in developing a consciousness in Tepoztecans of being Morelenses. After the Revolution, the state of Morelos developed an intense political life and during the thirties a constitutional government was established. This meant that the governor and local officials were to be elected rather than imposed and that political campaigns and electioneering inevitably developed. State candidates devoted a great deal of attention to nearby Tepoztlán. In their attempts to obtain votes they appealed to a sense of state loyalty, sometimes using such slogans as "First the Morelenses and then the Mexicans."

The state of Morelos has its own civic fiestas which are celebrated with considerable flourish. Among the most important are the celebration of the birthday of Father Morelos, after whom the state was named, and celebrations of the birth and death of Emiliano Zapata, the most popular hero. As in the case of national holidays, the school is the organizing and driving force. The teachers and the school director, for example, give speeches reviewing the great achievements of Zapata and point out that five of his generals were Tepoztecans. Tepoztecans also send delegations to the official state celebration of Zapata's birthday. A few small newspapers published in Cuernavaca occasionally reach Tepoztlán but these are read chiefly by courthouse officials. Regional songs with lyrics about the state of Morelos are known to the villagers.

Tepoztecans fear and respect the power and authority of the state government. They fear the public jails and courts of Cuernavaca and the police officials who occasionally come to the village to make arrests or track down offenders. They have aversion for the state office of rents which collects the bulk of the village land taxes. Although the tax rate is very low, the state collected over sixty thousand pesos in the twelve years from 1931 to 1943, according to the official state tax records in Cuernavaca. During this same period the only state funds which were returned to the village was the salary of the state tax collector who was paid on a pro-rate basis. The *Procuradia* of the state handles property cases and summons Tepoztecans to appear in Cuernavaca for hearings. The villagers complain that this agency will summon them during the height of the agricultural season just as readily as at any other time. The governor is recognized as an important figure and is known by name to many villagers; indeed, some of them remember the names of the governors of the Díaz epoch. Tepoztecans tend to be more critical of the state than of the federal government and are less hesitant about sending a delegation to the governor than to the president.

The Village and the Municipio

The municipio is the functional resource unit for the villagers, and hence the relations of the village with the municipio are closer and more personal than those with any of the larger units discussed so far. Tepoztecans know the municipio intimately; they know its geography, history, legends, natural resources, people, and villages. Even small children can name the seven surrounding villages and know how to find their way to each one. The limits of the municipio and the details of the many recurring boundary disputes with neighboring municipios are also well known. Village boundaries are vague, essentially moral boundaries, but municipal boundaries are clearly demarcated. It is within these bounds that the Tepoztecan has his everyday world. Here he works the communal lands, cuts and burns communal forests, grazes his cattle, and hunts for medicinal herbs.

The municipio extends for about seventeen miles from the ragged mountains and heavily wooded country of the north down the slope of the Ajusco mountain range to the level, fertile lands of the sugar plantations near Yautepec. From the northern limits to the southern limits the drop in altitude is from about 10,500 feet to about 3,700. Although most of the villages cluster near the center of the municipio, they are located at seven different levels. The widest range is between San Juan in the north at about 7,000 feet and San Andrés in the south at about 4,300 feet. San Juan is 2,000 feet above Tepoztlán, although the villages are less than four miles apart.

The northern part of the municipio lies in *tierra fría,* or the cold zone; the middle part in *tierra templada,* or the temperate zone; and the southern part in *tierra caliente,* or the hot zone. San Juan, the highest village, is at the lower limit of the *tierra fría,* while San Andrés, the lowest village, is at the upper limit of *tierra caliente.* Three of the villages, Tepoztlán proper, Ixcatepec, and Amatlán, are at approximately the same level in the temperate zone. The villages each have a distinctive flora and some depend on charcoal production more than on agriculture. In San Juan, for example, there is little crop land, no coffee trees, no hog plums, and no tropical or semitropical fruits. But unlike the other villages, San Juan grows a little wheat and barley, and some potatoes, and produces a great deal of charcoal. It also has fruit orchards of peaches, pears, *capulin,* and *tejocote.* Each of the villages brings its products to the Tepoztlán market, thus making for interdependence within the municipio.

The territorial unit which is today the municipio was already a sociopolitical unit in pre-Hispanic times and is therefore much older than either the state of Morelos or the nation. According to legend, the surrounding villages were originally defensive military outposts of the central village of Tepoztlán where political control rested.

The bonds between Tepoztlán and the surrounding villages of the municipio are numerous. The strongest bonds are the communal lands and the biweekly market at Tepoztlán. Administratively, Tepoztlán is the center in which all municipal births, marriages, and deaths must be registered, taxes paid, and certificates of good conduct obtained. The other villages also are dependent on Tepoztlán for their religious services, baptisms, communions, Mass, and confession, for only Tepoztlán has a resident priest. On fiesta occasions a great deal of intervillage visiting occurs. Ties of marriage within the municipio, however, are relatively weak; only about a dozen persons from the other villages have married into Tepoztlán and cases of Tepoztecans going to live in the surrounding villages are practically unheard of. Ties of *compadrazgo* establish bonds between the villages of the municipio, but Tepoztlán's dominant position again is revealed by the fact that while other villagers seek out Tepoztecans to act as godparents for their children, Tepoztecans do not reciprocate.

That Tepoztecans feel superior is shown further by their characterizations of other villagers. The people of Ocotitlan are described as "dangerous," "violent," "assassins"; the people of Gabriel Mariaca as *tontos* or fools, wealthy but backward Indians. The women of Gabriel Mariaca are scorned because they work in the fields, wear straw hats, and carry heavy loads "like men." Some of the traditional Nahuatl nicknames for the surrounding villagers also are indicative of Tepoztecan attitudes: Gabriel Mariaca people are referred to as *cuatlateme* (dull heads) and those from La Calera as *cuatichtizatin* (white-headed people because they make lime).

The political dominance of Tepoztlán over the surrounding villages is clear. Although in theory, any male adult from any one of the eight villages of the municipio may become president of the municipal government, in practice he is almost always a Tepoztecan.

In recent years, conflicts over communal lands have set village against village and have seriously weakened municipal bonds. Competition which had not existed before arose when an increasing exploitation of communal resources for commercial rather than for subsistence purposes was encouraged by the coming of the railroad and the highway, and by a greater need for cash. The outlying villages finally demanded sole rights of control over the communal lands adjoining them. In effect they were insisting that moral boundaries be accepted as legal ones, in which case the communal municipal lands would be interpreted as village lands. The most serious quarrel flared up in the early twenties when the village of San Juan took advantage of the fact that the railroad ran through the village; since the railroad could transport charcoal, San Juan began to develop its charcoal industry on a commercial scale. The authorities of Tepoztlán at once challenged the right of San Juan to exploit municipal resources for the benefit of a single village. The dispute was bitter and led to violence. In the end, federal authorities had to intervene.

The Village

The physical aspects of the village, the population, language, housing, diet, clothing, and recreation have been described in earlier pages. Here we are concerned with Tepoztlán's social structure: the extent of village solidarity and identification, and the role of such village-wide organizations as the school, the market, the church, and the local government.

The village is a corporate body which enjoys legal status: it can sue and be sued in the courts. It is an administrative unit and most of the social, economic, and religious activities of the villagers take place within it. The stability of residence and the predominance of endogamous marriages (over 90 percent of all marriages are made within the village) encourage village identification, a trend which is further enhanced by the absence of well-developed class distinctions. Because each family, rich or poor, owns a house and housesite and has recognized status as a villager, each villager can proudly say "This is my village and the village of my ancestors." The sense of identification with the village is clearly apparent in those who have left it to live in Mexico City. Early in the twenties the emigrants formed a *Colonia Tepozteca* which still exists and which works in behalf of village interests. Further, many Tepoztecans in Mexico City maintain their ties with the village, visit regularly at the *Carnaval* or other fiestas, and express a wish to die and be buried in their home village. There is considerable verbalization about village community spirit. Political candidates always speak of *mi pueblo* and promise to improve the village. That once in office they may in fact do very little and are often accused by the villagers of stealing funds does not reduce the importance of village loyalty as an ideological factor that is potentially unifying.

The local government, located in the central plaza, is the most definitive expression of the village as an organized unit. The *ayuntamiento* or governing body consists of the president, the *síndico* or law enforcement officer, the *regidor* in charge of finances, and the secretary. In addition, there are the treasurer, the police chief, a sub-police chief, a judge, a secretary to the justice, and a porter. Eight *ayudantes* or delegates represent the eight *demarcaciones* into which the village is divided for governmental purposes. The president, *síndico, regidor,* and judge are elected for a two-year period. The other officials are appointed by the president in conjunction with the *síndico* and *regidor.*

The duties of the major officials are determined by state law. The president is the executive officer and the official representative of the village in its contacts with the outside. His signature is necessary for most correspondence and official acts, and he fixes the fines imposed for infractions of the law. Some of the villagers also bring their private difficulties to him—quarrels between neighbors and between husbands and wives, and litigations over property, and so forth. By far the greatest number of tasks, however, falls to the secretary of the local government who is generally the most literate of the officials. In the period from 1943 to 1948, the secretary was a competent typist, an unusual accomplishment in the village.

Salaries paid to government officials are very low even by Tepoztecan standards; the daily salary of the president is lower than the prevailing wage rate for a day laborer. Such low salaries encourage *la mordida* (the bite) or graft. The major sources of local government income are taxes from the slaughter of animals, payments in lieu of rendering public service, exemption of publication of acts in the public register, and taxes from the use of the communal lands. From 1940 to 1943, the average annual income of the government was about seven thousand pesos, a sum which covered salaries only and left nothing for public improvements. Lack of funds is one of the most demoralizing aspects of the local government, and Tepoztecans look to the federal government for help with the problem. It should be noted that the village and the municipio derive practically no income from land taxes, most of which accrue to the state government.

Public works such as improving roads and constructing public buildings are organized by the village authorities through the village *cuatequitl*, an ancient form of collective labor. Every able-bodied man between the ages of twenty-one and fifty-one is obliged to contribute twelve days a year in work. Failure to appear for service is punishable by fine or a jail sentence. A man may pay for a substitute, however, and a few of the better-to-do families prefer to do this because they consider some of the work below their dignity. The poor who cannot afford substitutes or fines are the main source of labor for the village *cuatequitl*. When the task is a relatively light one and more men are called up than are needed for the actual work, some may be asked to contribute food or drink instead of labor.

In recent years there have been relatively few *cuatequitls* of major importance but the tradition is always ready in case of an emergency. In 1925-27 the village washbasins were constructed during a socialistically oriented administration; in 1934 the village market place was improved. In the early thirties, a time when the village was split into two hostile political factions, an impressive demonstration of collective labor occurred in connection with the construction of the road to Cuernavaca. Led by two enterprising non-Tepoztecan school teachers and backed by the *Colonia Tepozteca,* the villagers decided to begin the road. The political factions known as the Bolsheviki and the Centrales refused to work side by side. Each then organized separate shifts, one beginning at Tepoztlán and working toward Cuernavaca and the other working from Cuernavaca to Tepoztlán.

The ability of the village authorities to organize the labor force of the village on crucial occasions is most impressive. In a recent boundary dispute with the municipio of Tejalpa, the authorities posted aides at all the roads and paths leading out of the village to intercept the men as they went out to their fields in the early morning. In this way six hundred men were recruited in one day to cut through the forest overgrowth and to re-establish a clear boundary between Tepoztlán and Tejalpa.

Although the village *cuatequitl* was intended as a means of benefiting the village as a whole, many obstacles have prevented its successful operation and it has been declining. The inherent individualism of Tepoztecans, their suspicious and critical attitude toward the local government, and the paucity of village funds all present difficulties. The villagers often criticize the *cuatequitl* as being a coercive rather than as a voluntary institution. Since the president and the *síndico* have the power to designate which citizens are to work in it, there is opportunity for favoritism and also for revenge against political opponents or personal enemies. It may be significant in this connection that when playing games, children will refer to the *cuatequitl* as a form of punishment. It should be noted also that historically this form of collective labor was a distinct aid to the Spanish conquerors in their organization and control of native labor.

The school, which was discussed earlier, is another important agency which helps create village-wide associations. Children from all the barrios meet at school and form friendships which tend to break down barrio localism; their parents sometimes serve on school committees. The stores, the corn mills, and the village market play a similar socializing function. Women from all parts of the village look forward to the exchange of news and gossip on their shopping trips.

Perhaps the most important single organizing and unifying factor on the village level is the central church. Catholicism with its village-wide festivals provides a common framework of symbols and ritual and brings the villagers together at the central church on all major holidays (see p. 13). The priest visits all the seven barrio chapels on special occasions. A number of religious associations are village-wide, among them the *Asociación Guadalupana*, the *Cofradia de la Virgen del Carmen*, the *Sagrado Corazón de Jesús*, and the *Acción Católica*. In 1948, the first three of these organizations each had a membership of about thirty women; the *Acción Católica* had a section of eighty boys and another section of thirty girls.

The Barrio

The village is divided into seven barrios or named locality groupings, each with its own chapel, patron saint, internal organization, and annual fiesta. The barrio is essentially a socioreligious organization with fixed boundaries and great stability; most of the present-day barrios were probably built up in the seventeenth and eighteenth centuries. The first mention of the contemporary barrios is found in a document of 1807 which is a census of the village by barrios and by the Nahuatl names of housesites within each barrio. It reveals that barrio boundaries have changed very little over the past hundred and fifty years. The names and the number of housesites of the present-day barrios are as follows: Santo Domingo, 174; San Miguel, 163; La Santísima, 139; Santa Cruz (large), 67; Los Reyes, 37; San Sebastian, 34; Santa Cruz (small), 29; and San Pedro, 19. With the omission of Santa Cruz (small) which, strictly speaking, is not yet an independent barrio, there are three large and four smaller barrios. The larger ones (Santo Domingo, San Miguel, and La Santísima) are grouped around the central plaza; the smaller ones are located above them on the mountain slope. Since the entire village is on a slope, the smaller barrios at the upper end are usually referred to as *los de arriba* and the larger ones at the bottom as *los de abajo*. Some Tepoztecans now refer to the paved road as the dividing line between the upper and lower halves of the village.

The barrios serve to break up the village into smaller communities which provide more opportunities for face-to-face relations. Kinship ties tend to be strongest within one's own barrio or with an adjoining one. As high as 42 percent of all marriages in a barrio occur among its own members; about 50 percent occur between persons of adjoining barrios. Most of the villagers in the smaller barrios of San Pedro, San Sebastian, and Los Reyes know each other by their first names and have considerable social interaction. The other barrios are much too large to be primary units. In all the barrios, however, most of the people have not visited the homes of any more than a dozen families in their barrio.

Barrio membership is determined mainly by ownership of a housesite in a barrio and by payment of a tax for the upkeep of the barrio chapel. In this fashion the barrio maintains its stability as a corporate unit despite any changes of residence that may occur. Since it is the housesite that traditionally belongs to one barrio or another, whoever lives on it, whether he obtains it by inheritance or by purchase, becomes a member of the barrio. Formerly, a housesite, especially in the smaller barrios, could not be sold without the agreement of the barrio members. A person usually belongs to the barrio in which he was born or raised, although a man who was born and raised in one barrio may purchase a housesite in another and establish his home there. If he pays the barrio tax and participates in the affairs of the barrio, he automatically becomes a member of the barrio where he now lives. He may for reasons of sentiment continue to support his barrio of origin and attend its fiestas, particularly if he still has relatives there, but this is voluntary.

A few persons own housesites in two or three barrios and pay taxes in each but consider themselves members of the barrio in which they live or where they were born and raised. Young couples sometimes buy a house in a barrio to which neither of them belongs and thereby acquire membership in a barrio new to both. Since patrilocal residence predominates, the men of any barrio are generally more closely related than the women. Upon marriage a woman becomes a member of her husband's barrio. Women more than men maintain dual barrio loyalties, however, and often return to their original home to help their parents prepare barrio fiesta meals.

Each barrio has a *mayordomo* who is responsible for the collection of funds for the upkeep of the chapel and for the organization of barrio members into collective work parties to clean the churchyard, repair the chapel or the streets, and help cultivate and harvest the corn on the plot of land belonging to the chapel. Preparing for the annual barrio fiesta is an extremely important job. The *mayordomo* decides how the fiesta is to be celebrated, whether to have a Mass or a sermon or both, and whether to invite a priest from Cuernavaca. He arranges for the band of musicians and for fireworks, and his family serves *mole, tamales,* and *ponche* to the guests, many of whom are from other barrios. Frequently he spends his own funds to assure a successful fiesta. Most of the expenses, however, are collected from barrio residents in the form of offerings or *limosnas;* these are considered a perpetual pledge to the saint of the barrio. The *mayordomo* appoints assistants and committees for specific assignments but he has no authority beyond his personal influence.

The selection of the *mayordomo* takes place in the barrio churchyard the evening before the Day of the Dead. Only the men participate. A bonfire is made, punch is served, likely candidates are discussed, and speeches in Nahuatl are made by the older men. The *mayordomo* is usually chosen by mutual agreement; there is no tradition of formal voting. Yet the selection of the *mayordomo* comes closer to a true expression of the people's will than does the election of the village officials. The village priest does not control the choice of the *mayordomo* although he considers the barrios to be his parishes.

To be eligible for the office of *mayordomo,* one must be a native of the village, a member of the barrio, and a married man, although there have been exceptions to the last requirement. A reputation for honesty and a willingness to serve the barrio are essential, for the position entails responsibility and expense. As a rule, the wealthier families do not seek the position but pressure is sometimes placed on them to accept. Formerly, the *mayordomo* was expected to serve for only one year, but in recent times a paucity of candidates especially in the smaller barrios has made it necessary for some *mayordomos* to hold office for as long as five years. Until recently, also, the position of *mayordomo* was considered a prerequisite for holding office in the local government, and a check of the members of the village council over the ten-year period from 1934 to 1943 showed that most of the presidents and *síndicos* of the local government had worked their way up through the job of *mayordomo.* This suggests an integration of secular and religious offices which is so characteristic of many Indian villages.

Important economic and social characteristics differentiate the barrios. On the whole, the smaller barrios are poorer and have a higher proportion of families that depend upon the communal lands, a higher incidence of illiteracy, and a reputation of being more Indian. San Sebastian is by far the poorest barrio, followed by San Pedro and Santa Cruz. Los Reyes is exceptional in that it has the highest proportion both of landholders and of large holdings. The larger barrios of the center, which show the widest extremes in poverty and wealth, have controlled the village politically: practically all the village presidents from 1922 to 1944 came from the three large barrios, and none from San Pedro or San Sebastian. Most of the *ejidal* authorities in the village have been selected from the central barrios, also, and the lion's share of the *ejido* land grants have gone to them.

Barrio *esprit de corps* is evidenced in interbarrio competition, especially at the annual *Carnaval,* and in the claims of superior miraculousness for some barrio saints over others. In the past, competitiveness was also evidenced in the traditional nicknames of the barrios which were believed to express an awareness of distinctive barrio personality. Thus Santo Domingo was called The Toads; La Santísima, The Ants; San Miguel, The Lizards; Santa Cruz and San Sebastian, *Cacomixtles;* Los Reyes, the Maguey Worms; and San Pedro, *Tlacuaches.* Nowadays these nicknames are rarely used and have little function in the community. *Esprit de corps* is at its height at the annual fiesta celebrated in honor of the barrio saint, which usually lasts from one to seven days. The chapel is decorated, candles are brought in ceremonially and burned, a *castillo* of fireworks is erected and burned, festal dishes are prepared, the ancient flute is played on the chapel roof, sacred dances and sometimes bullfights are held, and a Mass is said in the chapel.

During the Díaz regime, distinctions between the larger and the smaller barrios corresponded to class distinctions much more so than at present. Since the Revolution the general tendency has been toward a decrease in barrio differences. The various barrios now participate much more equally in village life. In contrast to 1926 when Redfield reported no letters arriving at the outlying barrios, by 1943 San Pedro and Los Reyes were receiving their share of the mail, and since that time this trend has been accentuated. Today contacts between the outlying barrios and the outside world are much less mediated through the center of the village.

Above, Mexican artist at his week-end village home.
Below, kitchen of a poor peasant's home.

5

The Family

TEPOZTLÁN is a family-centered community. The biological family, the predominant type, consists of parents and unmarried children and constitutes the basic production unit of the village. Families in Tepoztlán are strong and cohesive, held together by traditional bonds of loyalty, common economic strivings, mutual dependence, the prospect of inheritance, and, finally, the absence of any other social group to which the individual can turn. Cooperation within the immediate family is essential, for without a family the individual stands unprotected and isolated, a prey to every form of aggression, exploitation, and humiliation known in Tepoztlán. It is within the small biological family that Tepoztecans seek personal security.

The extended family provides some additional security, particularly in times of emergency. It is characterized by a limited reciprocity of cooperation which includes borrowing and labor exchange. No institutionalized day-to-day cooperative endeavors exist between families, related or unrelated, however, and as a rule little aid is given or received. Visiting among relatives is surprisingly infrequent; it is limited to such special occasions as the annual barrio fiesta, illnesses, births, weddings, and deaths.

Over 70 percent of the 662 village housesites are occupied by the simple biological family, only 16 percent by multiple families. Most of the latter consist of parents living with their unmarried children and also with a married son and his family. There are some cases of a married daughter living with her parents and of married siblings sharing a common housesite. The number of persons per housesite ranges from 1 (45 cases, mainly widows or widowers) to 17 (1 case), with smaller households more numerous than larger ones. Most housesites hold a single house, although some have two, three, or four.

Several factors reveal a patriarchal emphasis in family organization: a principle of male superiority (husband over wife, brothers over sisters), a strong preference for patrilocal residence, and patrilineal descent. Tepoztecans are deprecatory of matrilocal residence, saying that when a young man goes to live with his wife's family after marriage "He was given away like a dog" or "He went as a male daughter-in-law." Nevertheless, over 20 percent of all married couples showed matrilocal residence. Most of the husbands in these cases were poor young men, either orphans or men who had married much older women or women of higher social and economic status. Each person in the village is known by the surnames of both his father and mother, but the latter is always given last and with successive generations is eliminated.

The nature of interpersonal relations within the family may perhaps best be understood if we examine them as they occur between husbands and wives, parents and children, among siblings, with the extended family, and with *compadres.*

Husbands and Wives

According to the ideal culture pattern for husband-wife relations in Tepoztlán, the husband is authoritarian and patriarchal; he is master of the household and enjoys the highest status in it. He is responsible for the support of the family and for the behavior of its members, and he makes all major decisions. It is his prerogative to be given obedience, respect, and service by his wife and children. The wife is expected to be submissive, faithful, and devoted to her husband, and to ask for his advice and permission before venturing on any but the most minor enterprises. She should be industrious and manage to save money no matter how small her husband's income. She should not be critical or jealous of her husband's activities outside the home nor even show any curiosity about them.

In most homes there is outward compliance to the ideal pattern, but few husbands are the dominant figures they seek to be and few wives are completely submissive. Many marriages reveal conflict on the question of authority and the roles of the spouses. The most even-tempered marriages are those which follow a middle course: the wife does little to challenge the authority of her husband and the husband is not too overbearing toward his wife.

Conflicts of this kind between husbands and wives are fostered by a basic discrepancy between actual roles and ideal roles in the organization of the family. Even though the wife is subordinate to her husband, it is she who has the central role within the house. She is responsible for planning, organizing, and managing the household, and for the training and care of the children. The husband traditionally turns over all his earnings to her. She is thus in a position to do a great deal of spending, borrowing, and paying back in secret, particularly since in most cases the husband does not interfere with her handling of the money so long as she gives some to him whenever he asks for it. The "good" wife should not refuse her husband's requests for money; if she does she may receive a scolding or a beating. The wife is free to sell small quantities of the family corn or her own chickens and eggs. She is supposed to obtain her husband's permission before going to a doctor or a *curandero,* visiting, or buying or selling in quantity, but the husband's frequent absences permit her to do many of these things without his knowledge.

The husband's actual participation in family and household affairs is minimal. His work is outside the home. The division of labor is clear-cut; except for emergencies and for such jobs as hauling water and repairing the house, the husband does not concern himself with the house or the children. The men are gone a good part of the day, sometimes for several days at a time depending on their work and the season of the year. In the past, Tepoztecan men worked in distant mines or on haciendas, and were absent from the village for long periods; before the Revolution, large numbers of men worked on nearby haciendas and returned home only once every two weeks. At present, about 150 men work on haciendas for from four to six months during the dry season, making visits to their homes once a week. With the husband away, the wife not only is head of the family but sometimes also has to support herself and the children.

Even more important perhaps than a husband's absence from his home are his behavior and attitude when he is at home. He avoids intimacy with the members of his family with the purpose of gaining respect from them. He holds himself aloof from the petty details of the household and expects to be undisturbed by complaints, requests, or noise. Unless he is told otherwise, he assumes that the home situation is as he wants it. Since wives are held accountable for everything that happens in the home, they tend to withhold information which might bring them disapproval or punishment. Thus, the loftiness of the husband's position tends to separate him from the very persons he is trying to control and inadvertently to give his wife and children the freedom he does not wish them to have.

In many homes the husband's sense of security is a function of the extent to which he can control his wife and children or make them fear him. Wife beating, more common in the past than now but still widespread, is resorted to for offenses that range from not having a good meal ready on time to suspicion of adultery. A jealous wife or a wife who objects to her husband's activities or judgment may also receive a beating. Wives are not expected to offer any resistance to the punishment. Wife beating is a recognized legal offense in the village but few wives report their husbands to the local authorities.

Tepoztecan women readily express hostility toward men and often characterize all men as "bad." Self-pity and a sense of martyrdom are common among married women, many of whom break down and cry when telling their life stories. As they grow older they often become more self-assertive and oppose their husband's attempts to limit their freedom and their business ventures. They begin to show preference for work outside the home and to feel deprived when they are tied down by housework and children. The present trend in the village is for the younger women and even the unmarried girls to take on the more independent attitudes of the older women.

Women are more in conflict with traditional ways than are the men.

Their standards of behavior for themselves and their husbands are changing; they veer between the old ideal roles and new needs and experiences. They readily admit to the superiority of men and tend to admire a man who is *macho* or manly, yet they describe the "good" husband as one who is not dominating but relatively passive. They also tend to regard the very submissive wife more as a fool than as an ideal. Apparently the women do not feel inadequate when they do not achieve the ideal of feminine behavior; indeed, they seem to feel pride rather than guilt in self-assertion.

Husbands often find themselves in a defensive position. They must conserve the old order of things if they are to maintain their control in the home, but the changes within the village in the past twenty years or so make this objective difficult. Such technological advances as the corn mills, the road, and the bus service to Cuernavaca have affected the women more than the men. An increasing number of the more ambitious married women now raise animals, or grow fruit on a larger scale, or sell family produce at the Tepoztlán and Cuernavaca markets. The more capable women are able to help their husbands substantially, in fact, without exception, every man who has prospered since the Revolution has done so with the help of his wife. Most men balk at permitting their wives to sell at the Cuernavaca market, however, despite the fact that the extra money would be welcome. In the past, this type of work was carried on exclusively by widows or women who "had no man to control them," and many of them were promiscuous and had little status. The fear of giving his wife more freedom and the subsequent threat to his role as provider are factors which prevent most men from allowing their wives to earn as much as they might.

Most young husbands are equally unprepared to give their brides of one or two years the freedom and authority they need to assume the responsibility for running independent households. In the past, when young wives lived with their mothers-in-law often for many years, their husbands had little difficulty in controlling them and felt correspondingly more secure. The men are unanimous in believing that women must be kept under strict surveillance if their good behavior is to be assured. Wives are generally forbidden to have female friends, for their husbands see such friends as potential go-betweens for the wife and a lover. Most women discontinue all friendships when they marry, and men may drop their own friends after marriage for fear that an intimacy might develop between the wife and the friend. The majority of husbands are suspicious of any activities that take the wife out of the home. A young wife will often prefer to ask a neighbor or a relative to buy things for her rather than risk her husband's anger or village gossip by going to the market alone. Some young wives now do go out alone but they are considered suspect.

In sexual relations as in social relations, the Tepoztecan husband is expected to take the initiative and his wife to submit to his demands. It is believed that women have less *naturaleza*—that is, that they are sexually weaker than men. Husbands do not expect their wives to be sexually demanding or passionate, nor do they consider these traits desirable in a wife. Women who "need" men are referred to as *loca* (crazy) and are thought to be in an abnormal condition which may have been brought about by black magic. Respectable women properly express negative attitudes toward sex and do so forcefully. Some husbands deliberately refrain from arousing their wives sexually, as it is assumed that a passive or frigid wife will be more faithful. In general, sexual play is a technique men reserve for the seduction of other women.

The husbands' concern about the faithfulness of their wives generally lessens after several years of marriage. As the children get older and can help the mother and as the needs of the growing family increase, however, women frequently demand freedom for carrying on economic ventures. Since such activity necessitates their leaving the house more often, tension and suspicion are again awakened in the husband. Men feel most secure when their wives are pregnant or have an infant to care for; thus to have one child follow close upon another is a desirable state of affairs from the men's viewpoint.

Promiscuous sexual activity is a male prerogative in Tepoztlán, and the men feel under pressure to prove their manliness by having many "affairs." Usually they have extramarital relations with widows or unmarried women, less frequently with married women. Men now go to houses of prostitution in Cuernavaca, and venereal disease is becoming more common in the village. Although male adultery is considered undesirable behavior, it is nevertheless thought to be "natural" and a good wife is not supposed to be disturbed by it. Many women are resentful, however, especially if money is involved, and some openly quarrel with their husband and also withhold money from him. Interference by wives in such matters enrages the men and often results in wife beating.

Drunkenness is not as common in Tepoztlán as it is in surrounding villages or in other parts of Mexico, and it is more strongly disapproved of. Most men drink a small amount of alcohol regularly, but extensive drinking is limited to Sundays, fiestas, or formal occasions. Drinking is nevertheless an important emotional outlet for Tepoztecan men; they drink to get over *muina* or anger after a quarrel at home, to work up courage to punish a wife, to seduce a woman, or to fight with an enemy. Sometimes when the men come home drunk they are aggressive and beat their wives; at other times "because they lack judgment" they are affectionate and kiss and fondle the members of their family. Many wives resent their husband's drunken bouts both because of the probable violence and because of the money involved; only the most aggressive, however, try to break their husband of the habit.

Tepoztecans believe that wives who have suffered beatings or other harsh treatment may take revenge through sorcery, and Tepoztecan men are alert to this possibility. The most commonly feared type of sorcery is a potion made from a well-known herb called *toloache*, secretly dropped into a man's coffee or any other drink. This herb is said to contain a drug that will affect the brain if taken in large doses. In Tepoztlán it is also believed that it will make a man *tonto*—that is, stupid or foolish and easily managed—and that an extra large dose will make him an idiot. The most important symptom to Tepoztecans is that the drugged man can no longer control his wife but is dominated by her. The man's mother or sister may attempt to cure him by secretly putting a counter-potion into his coffee. It is interesting to note that there is not a single known case of *toloache* given by a man to a woman.

Parents and Children

Tepoztecan children are brought up to obey their elders and to submit to the will of their mother and father as long as they live under their parents' roof. From infancy on, they are encouraged to be passive and unobtrusive; older children are expected to be self-controlled and helpful. Great emphasis is placed on "good" behavior in children, for it is feared that a child improperly raised will not grow up to be a good worker and will get into trouble. Such a son or daughter is a cause for shame to his parents in the eyes of the community.

The mother is expected to teach the children good habits and to see to their religious training. As far as the children are concerned, family life revolves primarily around the mother. At an early age they learn not to expect to be held by their father or to have much physical contact with him. In many homes the father rules the children through the mother who then becomes the mediator between father and children, relaying requests, instructions, and warnings. The father expects the mother to help maintain his position of respect in the home, and in this most women comply. Children are repeatedly warned by relatives and other adults that the father must be respected. Most children are subdued and inhibited in the presence of their father and remain so well into adulthood. They are less consistent in their behavior toward their mother, thus reflecting her own varying attitudes, for she is at the same time punishing and protective, authoritative and submissive, serving and demanding.

Popular stereotypes in the village depict fathers as "hard" by nature and the mother as "soft." It is thought natural that a mother feels closer to her children than does the father; a mother who abandons her children is considered abnormal or *machorra* (like a man). When a man deserts his children—a more common occurrence—it is disapproved of but not considered a sign of abnormality. Again, the death of a mother is recognized as more disruptive to the household than the death of a father.

According to village culture patterns a mother has more ways of showing affection to her children than a father. She may kiss, fondle, or carry a nursing child as much as she wishes, and if a child is the youngest she may continue this behavior until he is five. She may also express affection through giving food, sewing clothes, nursing illness, and other attentions. Mothers often protect their children by not telling the father of misdeeds or by attempting to stop the father from punishing a child. Such interventions and deceptions are infuriating to the father, but they are nevertheless thought to be "natural" in a mother. In contrast to the mother, a father is limited in his ability to be demonstratively affectionate with his children. Traditionally, a father expresses his affection by buying a child little gifts, giving him pennies, or taking him to the fields or to a fiesta. When a child is ill, the father shows his concern chiefly by agreeing to call in a *curandero*.

Our data show a wide variation in the form and severity of punishments meted out to children. This situation stems from the varying amount of help needed from children in the home and from the differential treatment given boys and girls, older and younger children, and a favorite child. A Tepoztecan child is always punished for flouting the authority of his parents and for unwillingness to work. Other types of misbehavior—grumbling or quarrelsomeness, for example—are not so consistently punished.

Most parents believe in early punishment and begin at about the time the child starts to walk. Infants may be slapped for crying too much, although this is uncommon. Some children receive their first severe beating at three or four years of age, but it is between five and twelve that children are most frequently and harshly punished. After twelve years, punishment is reserved for the most serious offenses. The father inflicts the most severe punishments but the mother punishes more often. Mothers tend to punish daughters more than sons; fathers punish sons more than daughters.

Severe punishment is traditional in Tepoztlán. Some adults in the village remember such punishments as hanging a child in a net over a smoky fire of chile seeds; partial asphyxiation and an illness that lasted for days was the result. (This practice is reminiscent of an ancient Aztec punishment which placed rebellious subjects in a room filled with the fumes of burning chile seeds.) Similarly, a child formerly was punished for breaking a dish by scraping his arms with a piece of the dish until blood was drawn. It is significant of changing attitudes in the village that some of the old practices which had a strong magical component and were not necessarily performed in a spirit of cruelty are today interpreted as cruel. Yet even today beatings with a stick or a rope are not uncommonly given by fathers. Mothers more often hit with their hands, pinch, kick, or throw small stones at offending youngsters. On the whole, Tepoztecans agree that punishment has become less severe and that there is greater toleration toward children's faults. This is particularly true among the more permissive and better-educated younger generation.

Fear is one of the most important means by which Tepoztecan parents control their children. Mothers threaten to desert their children, playing on their fear of being orphans or of having to live with a stepmother. In the days when few visitors or tourists came to the village, children were told that if they were naughty they would be carried off by a stranger who would make them into soap. In the more isolated villages children still run to hide when they see an unfamiliar person. Many mothers and grandmothers tell young children stories of owls and coyotes that come out at night to eat bad children, and of bats and opossums that drink blood. Children who lie or disobey are warned that they will turn into devils and burn in hell. When children cry they may be told the story of Cahuasohuantun who eats the intestines of such children.

Lying and deception play a large part in parent-child relationships. Parents and other adults use deception as another means of controlling children; Tepoztecans actually would be at a loss in raising their children if they were without it. The use of little lies is so common as to be taken for granted, and children early become accustomed to it. Mothers, particularly, tend to make and break promises easily and to trick their children into doing as they wish. The effort of parents to keep their children "innocent," or, as they say, "to keep their eyes from being opened," makes deception necessary. Children, in turn, lie to escape punishment and to assert their own wishes. Moreover, the many restrictions placed upon children encourage lying; there is, for example, much deception involved in courtship. Parents show little moral indignation about lying on the part of their children. They do not punish the lie so much as the misdeed the lie was meant to hide; likewise, a parent or child caught in a lie is ashamed rather of being caught than of having lied.

The frequent use of deception causes some mutual distrust between parents and children. The children seldom confide in their parents, and early stop going to them for help with their troubles or for information. The parents on their part do not encourage the asking of questions, particularly about sex. Absurd or teasing answers are often given to children's questions.

The father assumes an important role in the life of a son when the boy is old enough to go to the fields. Most boys enjoy working in the fields with their father and look forward to it with great pleasure. Fathers are proud to take their young sons to the fields for the first time and frequently show great patience in teaching them. But even when father and sons go to the fields together day after day, there is no weakening of the respect relationship. The father maintains the role of teacher and when he speaks it is to advise. Talk between them about intimate subjects, the telling of jokes, or discussion of women all are strictly taboo, even after the sons are married.

Regardless of age or marital status a son is subject to his father's authority as long as he lives with his father. He receives no recompense other than his support and care and whatever spending money he can manage to procure. Some fathers are generous with sons who do a man's work; others continue to treat them as children. In the past, comparatively few unmarried sons left home to seek work elsewhere; even young men who were acutely dissatisfied with their home situation were reluctant to strike out for themselves. A certain apprehension of the outside world still holds sons at home—fears of falling ill among strangers, of having to do menial work, of not having the family to support them in case of trouble, of not being properly respected by others. Moreover, many boys feel bound to their mothers. Still another factor that prevents sons from leaving home is their economic dependence on their parents and a desire for their share of the inheritance. The dependence is, of course, mutual. Fathers are eager to have their sons at home to help support the family, and in most homes grown sons who work enjoy much the same service and care that the father receives.

Although fathers say they prefer sons to daughters, they not uncommonly show a mild favoritism toward a daughter. Relations between a father and a grown daughter are formal and distant, however, and physical contact is avoided. Kissing and embracing have strong incestuous connotations for both.

Even young girls are extremely shy in the presence of their fathers and some married women say they are embarrassed at being seen by their father when they are pregnant. Fathers expect their daughters to be virgins when they marry. Any violation of this moral law is a blot on the father's and on the family's honor and incurs severe punishment.

Mothers more than fathers tend to have favorites among their children; usually they favor boys over girls and small children over grown children. Many mothers try to protect their sons if they think the father works them too hard, but only an occasional mother will interfere in the boy's behalf. It is common for a mother to be indulgent with her youngest child; she may nurse him and sleep with him much longer than the usual period. The indulgence of the youngest child is often in sharp contrast with the treatment of the older children, but generally speaking mothers give partial treatment to all children under five. The small children are given more food and toys and are taken to fiestas and on trips. Although differential treatment of children according to sex and age is "accepted" as natural by Tepoztecan parents, there is evidence that habitual or gross displays of favoritism are resented by the other siblings. The resentment finds expression in surreptitious quarreling and fighting, in irritability, in unwillingness to share possessions, and in avoidance of one another.

From early childhood, boys are permitted more freedom of movement and of expression and more leisure for play than girls. The oldest son enjoys a particularly favored position. He receives more care and attention than subsequent sons, and his is often the only birthday other than the father's to be celebrated with a fiesta. But mothers sometimes have difficulty controlling the oldest son, for the boy may imitate his father in demanding service from the women of the family and in giving orders to the younger siblings. If the father dies, the oldest son is expected to take the father's place and to support his mother, brothers, and sisters. An extended struggle for authority as head of the family sometimes ensues between mother and son. Quarrels between mother and son about the inheritance also are apt to arise. Widows who inherit their husband's property have an advantage in the matter of maintaining authority and usually they keep the property until their death lest they lose all control over their sons.

Relations between mothers and daughters are usually very close. As the mother teaches the girl household skills and as they work side by side in the home, the daughter comes to identify with the mother and assume her role. A daughter's attitudes toward work, toward bearing children, and toward men and marriage are strongly influenced by her mother. The custom of having daughters work in the home is a deeply ingrained one, and a girl at home is at the complete disposal of her mother. With few exceptions mothers use their daughters very early for all types of errands and chores. Mothers tend to resent the fact that school takes the girls away from home for the major part of the day, and most parents remove their daughters from school as soon as they can. The majority of girls attend school only through the third grade or until they are eleven. Many mothers exploit their daughters, particularly the oldest, and some girls marry to escape the hard work at home. An occasional mother, however, identifies with her daughter and fulfills her own desire for schooling by allowing the girl to complete elementary school.

A mother is responsible for the chastity and reputation of her grown daughters. To many mothers this translates into a need to spy on them, to chaperone them, and to put pressure on them to conform. If a mother learns that a daughter has a *novio,* she may beat the girl herself rather than inform the father. If, however, a daughter becomes pregnant before marriage, the mother will usually be less harsh and more forgiving than the father. Respect relations between a mother and a daughter forbid them to speak of intimate subjects although not to the same extent as father-daughter relations. Mothers usually do not give their daughters information about menstruation nor discuss the body or any aspect of sexual relations with them. Nor do girls tell their mothers when they first menstruate or ask for information concerning pregnancy, birth, or marriage. When a mother learns that a daughter has begun to menstruate or is pregnant, however, she will offer advice. Mother-daughter relations are considerably weakened when a girl marries, particularly if the girl lives with her mother-in-law. If she leaves her mother-in-law to establish a home of her own, close relations with her mother are usually resumed. Women do not expect financial help from their married daughters but many do receive such help with or without the knowledge of their sons-in-law.

Siblings

Sibling solidarity is an ideal which parents hold before their children and to which lip-service is constantly given. In childhood, siblings are constant companions, sharing the same friends and the same games. The older children take care of the younger and are held responsible for their safety and well-being but they may not discipline them or exercise much authority over them. If a younger child cries or complains to the parents, the older child is scolded or punished. As a result, older children rarely run to their mothers with complaints or appeals for justice but younger children frequently do so. In the school, however, older children vent their aggression upon younger ones to such an extent that parents are reluctant to send small children to kindergarten.

The oldest sister in particular has the role of caring for the younger siblings and often shows maternal affection toward them; a newly-weaned child may sleep with her for several years. Some older daughters are now rejecting this role, however; they prefer to go to school and tend to be resentful if they cannot. The oldest brother has preferred status and can demand respect and obedience from younger siblings even though the parents try to frustrate his efforts in this direction unless or until he is an adult. The general pattern of male dominance, learned by boys from their fathers, is first put into practice in their relationships with their sisters. As soon as a girl is old enough to do housework, the brother begins to demand service from her just as his father does from his mother. A sister is expected to wash, iron, and mend her brother's clothes, prepare and serve his food, and so forth. Like their father, boys have a lively concern about their sister's "honor" and will beat her if they discover she has a *novio*.

Siblings of the same sex tend to associate with each other. Brothers work in the fields together, share confidences, and if there is no great age difference between them, share the same friends. This pattern is even stronger among sisters. Grown brothers and sisters, however, do not attend fiestas or other public affairs together, do not have mutual friends, and are reserved toward one another in public.

Many brothers and sisters, of course, have warm relationships throughout their lives, but in many families sibling relations are poor. Among infants and young children, sibling rivalry and jealousy are so common that parents think them natural and take them for granted. Children are not prepared for the arrival of a new sibling and the pregnancy and birth are kept a secret from them. An illness (called *chipilez*) that occurs in infancy is attributed to the child's jealousy of a new sibling. Even before the next baby is born, an illness in a nursing child or in a child being weaned is ascribed to jealousy. It is believed that infants "sense" when another child is expected and that the illness is caused by the fact that they are now "carrying the weight of the baby." Although death from *chipilez* is not infrequent, most children recover a few months after the new baby is born, since then, it is said, "the weight is lifted." If a child continues to cry for his mother and to show hostility to the new baby, he may be sent to live with his grandmother either temporarily or for as long as several years. Temper tantrums, common in the next-to-the-youngest child, also may be stopped in this way. Sometimes a youngest child is the butt of older siblings and for his own protection may be sent to live with his grandmother. The importance of the grandmother as a mother substitute is generally recognized in the village; the child who does not have a grandmother is considered unfortunate.

After marriage a number of factors weaken ties between siblings. Each brother or sister sets up an independent household, often widely separated, and in Tepoztlán practically no institutionalized forms of cooperation exist between married brothers and sisters. As we have seen earlier, only fourteen cases of married siblings living together on a single housesite were noted. Married sisters soon identify with their husband's interests. Moreover, since a married woman is under the authority of her husband, she is no longer free to visit her brothers at will. Brothers are more free to visit, but often there are strained relations between in-laws.

Again, favoritism on the part of the parents toward one or two married children may cause friction among adult siblings. For example, parents may show marked preference for a daughter's children or help a favored married daughter or son more than their other children. Division of inheritance also leads to quarrels among siblings; parents tend to leave more property to sons than to daughters, more to an older son, or to a favorite.

The Extended Family

During the time a married couple lives with the husband's parents, they have little contact with the wife's family. When they live alone, ties with the wife's family become closer and often supersede those with the husband's family. In any case, however, the closest kinship tie is with the grandmother, whether on the paternal or the maternal side. The importance of the grandmother, especially as a mother substitute, has already been pointed out.

Aunts, particularly maternal aunts, frequently have an affectionate relationship with nieces and nephews and in emergencies may act as mother substitutes. A boy who has eloped often brings his sweetheart to live with a favorite aunt. Uncles have a respect relationship with their nieces and nephews which may also be an affectionate one. Many children have a favorite uncle who singles them out for an occasional gift or favor. Work exchange between uncles and nephews occurs more often than between married siblings, but quarrels also are apt to occur, particularly over inheritance. After a man's death, a brother will sometimes claim a portion of the property from the widow, especially if her children are still small.

Cousins often have a relationship that resembles that of brother and sister. Parents encourage their children to play with their cousins, especially if they are neighbors; often a person's best and only friends turn out to be one or two favorite cousins. Cousin marriage is forbidden although some cases have occurred.

In-laws

Because of patrilocal residence, the mother-in-law and daughter-in-law relationship is the most important of all in-law relationships. When a young bride goes to live with her husband's family, she is expected to take the role of a grown daughter and give her parents-in-law the same respect and obedience she gave her own parents. The mother-in-law assigns her work to her; generally it consists of the most burdensome tasks—grinding corn, making tortillas, and washing and ironing clothes for the entire family. In the past, when girls married at twelve or thirteen, they were unskilled and the mother-in-law taught them housework. The mother-in-law for her part must look after her daughter-in-law when she gives birth and must chaperone the daughter-in-law and see to it that she remains a faithful wife. Many jokes depict the mother-in-law as a "policeman."

Although many mothers-in-law and daughters-in-law manage to get along fairly well, the relationship is a charged one and is recognized as such by Tepoztecans. Both women approach it with apprehension. Girls hear their mothers and other married women say that the daughter-in-law is the mother-in-law's "slave." They are afraid that they will not be able to please their mother-in-law and that they will feel like an outsider in a strange house. The mother-in-law fears that the girl her son brings home will be lazy, just another mouth to feed, or that she will be critical of the way the family lives.

Often the fears are justified and quarrels are the result. Perhaps this is even more true today than in the past because of the different standards of dress, cleanliness, and personal freedom held by younger and older women. Increasingly, the way out of an unpleasant situation for both is to separate the households. If the wife cannot persuade her husband to move and if her situation becomes intolerable, she returns to her parents' home. It is believed in the village that many marriages have been broken because the mother-in-law and daughter-in-law could not get on together. Father-in-law and daughter-in-law relations are similar to father-daughter relations but even more reserved.

Relations between the wife's parents and their son-in-law depend more on personal factors than on formal obligations, with the exception of the usual respect obligations. In the past, the son-in-law was required to provide his father-in-law with wood and water for two years as part of the bride price. Now any work done by the son-in-law is voluntary and usually is limited to times when the father-in-law is ill or in need. If the mother-in-law is widowed and has property, the son-in-law may help her farm; if she has no means of support, a good son-in-law may help support her or invite her to live in his home.

Tepoztecan men are wary of their mothers-in-law. They think of her as a meddlesome, trouble-making figure and prefer to keep the relationship a distant one. Actually, most mothers urge their married daughters to try to please their husbands and to bear up under domestic difficulties. Fathers are more apt than mothers to feel a personal affront if their daughter is ill-treated by a son-in-law.

Relations between sisters-in-law and brothers-in-law are not formalized and depend largely on personal factors. Sisters-in-law, whether the wives of two brothers or the husband's wife and sister, are thrown together more often than brothers-in-law. In some families the wives of brothers compete for the esteem of the mother-in-law and carry tales about each other to her. Quarrels over inheritance involve the sisters-in-law as much as the siblings.

Godparents, Godchildren, and Co-parents

The system of *compadrazgo* establishes two sets of formal relationships between nonrelatives: the one is between "spiritual" godparents (*padrinos*) and their godchildren (*ahijados*); the other a relationship known as *compadres* or co-parents, is between the parents and the godparents. The general purpose of godparents is to provide security for the godchild. The godparents are in effect an additional set of parents who will act as guardians and sponsors of the godchild, care for him in emergencies, and adopt him if he is orphaned. In Tepoztlán, however, the relationship between *compadres* is much more functional and important than that between the godparent and godchild.

Godparents address their godchildren in the familiar *tu* and are addressed by the respectful *Usted*. Traditionally the godchild kissed the godparent's hand at each meeting, but this is no longer common. The godparent usually gives the child a few centavos when they meet, but many children actually never receive anything from their *padrinos. Compadres* address each other with the respectful *Usted;* theirs is a reciprocal respect relationship and in this lies its strength, for such a relationship is highly desirable to Tepoztecans. By respect, Tepoztecans mean a recognition of high and equal status and the avoidance of intimacy or undue familiarity. The latter includes joking and discussing sex or any other subjects of a personal nature. Compadres also may not drink together. They do often exchange favors, and borrowing between them is probably more frequent than between kin. At the death of one *compadre* the other is supposed to contribute toward the funeral expenses. *Compadres* invite each other to barrio fiestas and treat each other with special deference. Tepoztecans prefer *compadres* who are neither neighbors nor relatives; most *compadres* come from other barrios.

The three most important types of godparents in Tepoztlán are those of baptism, confirmation, and marriage. Reliable persons are sought as godparents of baptism. The husband's parents usually select the godparents of baptism for the first child, but as the couple grows older the husband may make the selection and often friendship rather than higher economic status dictates his choice. The godparents of baptism are obliged to assist at the baptism, to buy the infant's clothing for the occasion, and to pay the priest's fee. They also accompany the mother and child to the *sacamisa,* or first Mass, forty days after the birth. If the child dies, the godparents arrange for the wake, dress the body for burial, and contribute to the funeral expenses. An important obligation of godparents is to urge their *compadres* to send the child to school when the time comes. If the child needs punishing, the parents may ask the godparents to scold him. The godparents of confirmation are usually selected by the godparents of baptism; occasionally the latter accept both roles. The godparents of marriage assist at the wedding and act as mediators if the couple later quarrels or separates.

One of the distinctive aspects of the *compadre* system in the village, and in fact in Mexico as a whole, is the way in which it has been extended far beyond the original Catholic forms. In most of Spain, only two or three types of godparents, popularly those of baptism, communion and confirmation, are known. In Tepoztlán, in addition to the three above, there are the following: godparents of *miscotón* (a Nahuatl term which refers to a small sweater which the godparent puts on the child to protect him from illness); of *medida* or *listón* (these terms refer to a small piece of ribbon, blessed by the priest, which is placed on a sick child as a charm); of *evangelio* (a woman of "bad" reputation is asked to become godmother to a sick child and to pray in the church for his recovery); of *scapulary;* of the Child Jesus; and so on. The godparent system has been extended to secular activities as well. At soccer and basketball games each team has its godmother who dresses in white, carries flowers, acts as the sponsor, and hands out prizes to the winners. At social dances godmothers act as chaperones.

Social, economic, and political factors may enter into the operation of the *compadre* system. Poor families look for better-to-do godparents for their children. Similarly it is thought desirable to have a *compadre* from the city, for it is assumed that a city family can be of greater help in time of need. The more godchildren a man has, the more *compadres* and the wider circle of persons who can be counted on for favors. For this reason anyone who aspires to a position of leadership in the village must have many godchildren. There is some feeling against using the *compadre* system in this fashion, however, and some villagers consider having many *compadres* as a burden. In this case they try to limit their *compadre* relations by asking one or two families to serve as godparents for several children.

6

The Life Cycle

Pregnancy

IN TEPOZTLÁN it is considered a sin for a married person not to want children or not to be grateful for all those sent by God. Children, it is emphasized, are economically useful and boys are preferred because they are economically more productive than girls. Women, however, tend to feel that having children is a burden to be endured and that bearing many children is a punishment from God. Not uncommonly they induce abortion and take medicines to cause sterility. The only approved method of avoiding conception in the village is abstinence. Tepoztecan men, however, prefer large families and frown on their wives' efforts to reduce the number of pregnancies.

Motherhood is not glorified. Girls grow up in a village atmosphere that indirectly encourages negative attitudes toward pregnancy, child bearing, and even marriage. There is prudery about pregnancy and women try to conceal it, especially from their children and from anyone in a respect relationship to them. The literal translation of the Spanish term used to describe pregnancy is "to become ill with child." When Tepoztecan girls married at an earlier age than they usually do at present, they were often ignorant of the signs of pregnancy for a sense of shame prohibited the giving of information by the mother to the daughter. Even today the young pregnant bride is dependent on her mother-in-law and a midwife for advice and care.

Sterility in women—which may be sufficient cause for abandonment by the husband—is believed to be caused by "cold" in the womb and is treated by massages with warm oil of rosemary and violet. It is also believed that if conception occurs during the full moon, the child will be strong, and married couples sometimes have intercourse during this time for this reason.

Care during pregnancy consists principally of abdominal massages given by a midwife. The patient lies down on her back with her knees slightly bent, and the midwife gently strokes the abdomen from right to left. No oils or unguents are used. It is thought that massage makes the birth easier and also allows the midwife to determine or even change the position of the fetus. Most women have great faith in the efficacy of massage and try to have it from two to four times a month. The midwife also advises the pregnant woman: she is not to lift heavy objects but she should continue to work, for too much sleep or rest would make the birth more difficult. She should not urinate where an animal has just urinated because the rising steam might cause inflammation of the womb. She should not bathe or wash clothes at the stream because *los aires* might endanger the child. Eclipses, rainbows, and earthquakes all are dangerous to an unborn child. No restrictions on sexual intercourse are made at any time during pregnancy. Miscarriages are generally blamed on the carelessness of the woman.

Birth

When the baby is expected, a curtain or *petate* is hung in front of the mother's bed. The woman lies on a *petate* on the floor and the midwife massages the abdomen, the back, and the hips with various heated oils. These are supposed to warm the infant, loosen it, and allow it to slip out more easily. Difficulty in giving birth is attributed to "cold" and is counteracted by heat. The woman is given a mixture of boiled herbs, chocolate, sherry, and egg to drink to hasten labor, or she is wrapped in a blanket to make her perspire. Sometimes leaves of *pericón,* rosemary, or laurel are burned in an old clay pot and the strong-smelling smoke is directed underneath the blanket to heat her lower body. The mother is discouraged from screaming during labor because, it is believed, this makes the child rise instead of descend. She is given something to bite on, usually her own braid, and is told to keep her mouth closed. It may be such practices which have led observers to describe Mexican Indian women as "stoical" during childbirth. Yet Tepoztecan women often pray and scream when they have severe pains.

After the child is born, a sash is wound around the upper part of the mother's abdomen to prevent the blood and the placenta from rising. The midwife may press a hot tortilla against the mother's right side or she may be given salt and onion to smell and mint to chew. When the afterbirth is expelled it is buried under the hearth. If it is carelessly disposed of or is eaten by a dog, the mother may die and the child's face may swell. The umbilical cord is cut with a scissors, tied with thread, and sealed with a few drops of tallow from a candle. The dried cord of a first-born son is believed to be an effective cure for certain eye diseases. A child born in a caul is destined to become rich and the caul is saved for good luck.

After the delivery, the mother is raised from the floor to a bed. The midwife binds her abdomen, tucking in a *muñeca* (literally, a doll), a piece of rolled up cloth, to add to the pressure and "fix the matrix." The mother's soiled clothing is removed and an old-fashioned Indian *huipil* made from a large square cloth is slipped over her head. A skirt made from another square is wrapped around her hips and legs. On the next day she is bathed and given her ordinary clothing.

The mother is kept on a restricted diet of corn gruel, cinnamon tea, and bread or tortilla until all flow of blood stops. The midwife massages and re-binds her every day for eight days to encourage the flow of blood and to "cleanse" her internally. The midwife also bathes the baby during her visits. If the mother's milk does not appear by the second day, several remedies are possible: the penis of an ox cut up and boiled, a gruel of sesame seed, chick peas, chocolate and cinnamon, or boiled *flor de pascua*. The first milk is considered harmful to the infant; it is expressed by hand and thrown on the ground or over the roof to prevent the mother's milk from drying up.

The care given to a new mother is striking. It consists of prolonged bed-rest (forty days is the ideal), freedom from household duties, sweatbaths, and abstention from sexual intercourse (for about one year). The prime motive is to delay another pregnancy as long as possible. Most women are glad to avoid intercourse, which they frequently call *abuso de hombre* (male abuse), and complain that their husbands do not wait long enough. The good husband and father owes it to both his wife and child to abstain. The husband is also supposed to hire a servant to help his wife for two or three months. Even among poor families, if the marriage has been consummated in church and approved by both families, women are well cared for after giving birth. This is not true for abandoned mothers, women without close relatives, or mothers of very large families.

The day after the birth close relatives come to the house with jars of food suitable for the mother. A week or two later more distant relatives come with food or perhaps with a gift of soap. Anyone who has recently attended a wake or a funeral should not come because he may expose the mother to a *mal humor* which causes "cancer" in menstruating women. Relatives who did not approve of the marriage usually stay away at this time.

For the first eight days the new mother remains behind the curtain. On the eighth day, if bleeding has stopped, she is carried by her husband or a hired man to the *temascal* for a sweatbath and then returned to her bed. After a minimum of fifteen days in bed, during which time she is urged to lie still without sitting up or turning from side to side, she is taken out for another sweatbath. Before each bath a special meal of *clemole* (chicken or beef cooked in a chile sauce) is eaten by the mother, the midwife, and any other women in the family. The new baby is briefly exposed also to the steam of the *temascal*. Almost every woman takes two steam baths; some take the traditional four. After the last bath, the mother may be given a boiled mixture of seventeen different herbs, and the same mixture is given to women who do not stop bleeding in good time. After leaving her bed, the mother is supposed to take precautions for two or three months—to sit quietly and to walk slowly with her thighs close together, and not to leave the house for at least forty days. Only the most unfortunate women do such heavy work as washing and ironing before three months have passed.

Many of the practices and beliefs pertaining to pregnancy and birth that are found in Tepoztlán are widespread in rural Mexico; they have been reported for Tarascan, Mayan, and Zapotecan groups. These similarities are due to contacts between these groups before the Conquest and to a common exposure to Spanish colonial influences.

Infancy and Early Childhood

No formal celebration is held at the birth of a child, for it is believed that during the first weeks of life the infant is particularly susceptible to "evil eye," "bad humors," and *los aires*. So that he can be protected from these dangers, the child sleeps behind a curtain, and *ruda,* chile, or a few drops of iodine are put in the cradle. Some families hang a gallstone, taken from the gall bladder of a bull, around the child's wrist to protect him from the "evil eye." After a month a centavo may be hung on a string around his neck to protect him from whooping cough. Babies in all families wear little caps for seven months to protect them from *los aires,* or, as more modern mothers say, from cold drafts, and they are generally kept indoors for the first four months.

Anyone coming in from the street must "cool" for awhile before seeing the baby because he may be "hot" and make the child ill. If the father has committed adultery and comes home "hot," his child may get infected eyes. Jealous wives sometimes accuse their husband of adultery if the child suffers any illness. Illness is also attributed to the fact that a child has weak *tonal* or *sombra;* this is something akin to a guardian spirit who protects him from disease. A very sick child may be treated by a *curandero* for spirit-loss.

Baptism usually occurs during the first week after birth. About forty days after the baptism the godparents present their godchild with a tray on which they have placed his baptismal clothes for the *sacamisa* or the first Mass attended by the mother and new baby. After the Mass the *compadres* visit the godparents with gifts of wine, cigarettes, turkey *mole,* and other festive foods. Later in the day the godparents may return the visit, bringing musicians and friends with them, and there will be dancing in the child's home. The *compadres* are obliged to serve food and drinks to all who come. The naming of children follows the Catholic custom of selecting one name from the list of saint's names on the day of birth and another, if desired, from the same list on the day of baptism.

Infants receive a good deal of attention and care and are generally kept fairly clean. Most babies under one year of age are bathed in warm water every three days, and most mothers handle them carefully and protect their eyes from soap. After the bath they are rubbed with alcohol, dusted with powder, and dressed in clean clothes. For the first three months the shirts and rag diapers are warmed at the hearth. Some mothers change soiled diapers often, others once a day or only after a bowel movement. Infants are traditionally swaddled, especially during nursing and sleeping, in a sheet or cotton blanket which binds their arms tightly down at their sides. This is done, it is said, to prevent the child from waking himself with a sudden movement of the hands which might cause *espanto* or illness of fright. It also prevents him from touching his genitals and from touching the mother's breast during nursing. Swaddling is considered an important part of child training, and its purpose is to make him more passive and quiet. It is believed that children who are bound in infancy will grow up to be less troublesome to the parents and not "turn out bad."

Infants are carried almost every waking moment up to the time they begin to walk; crawling on the ground is permitted only by "careless" mothers. Thus a well-brought-up child has little opportunity to explore. The baby is carried in the left arm, with one end of the *rebozo* or shawl tightly tucked around his body, and the other end brought around the mother's shoulders and also tucked under him. This makes him snug and also takes some of his weight off the mother's arm. Children are not slung in a *rebozo* on the mother's back as in some parts of Mexico, for Tepoztecans regard this method of carrying a child as primitive and as indicative of poverty—a poor woman needs both hands free to work. Most Tepoztecan women have someone to help them —an older child, a grandmother, some other relative, or a young girl hired for the purpose. The practice of entrusting an infant from the age of four months on to a child-nurse is general in the village.

During the day babies sleep in a shallow wooden cradle which hangs from the ceiling by a rope. The baby's face is covered with a cloth to protect him from *los aires* and to keep out light and flies. Cradles can be raised to safeguard the child from animals or lowered to prevent a high fall. Babies may be rocked to sleep in the cradle but most of the time they fall asleep in the mother's arms while nursing and are then placed in the cradle. At night babies sleep with their mothers on a *petate* on the floor or on a raised native bed or *tepexco*. If the mother sleeps on a modern bed, the child will be heavily wrapped at night to prevent wetting the mattress.

The baby is nursed whenever he cries. The breast is used as a pacifier and most babies are put to sleep in this way. Because nursing is considered good for the child and because it is believed to delay conception, mothers nurse as long as possible, usually until they are pregnant again. Tepoztecan women say they do not find nursing pleasurable, however, and consider it rather as part of a mother's sacrifice for the good of her child. Children who are nursed less than eighteen months are considered deprived.

Infants are not permitted to cry, for a crying child is thought to be hungry, neglected, or ill. If a crying baby is not consoled by the breast, the leaf of the *sapote blanco* or of the *dormidera,* a flower which closes when touched, is sometimes placed under the child's pillow. If the crying still does not stop, the child may be treated for *espanto*.

Children are not hurried in their development. If walking is seriously delayed, earth warmed by the sun may be rubbed on the legs to remove the "cold" in the bones. If a child cannot speak by the time he is three or four, a church key may be turned in his mouth to "unlock" it. It is believed that a child's fingernails should not be cut until he begins to speak because otherwise the palate will fall and he will be mute. It is also believed that a child's hair should not be cut before one year or he will become ill. When teeth come late, older people may advise bleeding the gums by rubbing them with a grasshopper's leg, but few young people now follow this practice. Some mothers put mittens on babies' hands to prevent them from scratching themselves.

There is little preoccupation with toilet training, particularly during the first two years. As soon as a child is able to walk, he is taken to the *corral* by his mother and is shown the proper place to relieve himself. He may be scolded or spanked even before he is two for doing his "necessities" in the wrong place, but most mothers are not consistent in this. When he is able to tie and untie his pants, usually by four or five, he is able to go independently.

Infancy ends with weaning. This is accomplished by placing a bitter substance (*sávila*) on the nipple and by telling the child that he cannot nurse any longer. Some women bind their breasts to stop the flow of milk and do not permit the child to see the breast again. Others do it more gradually, letting the child nurse if he cries too much. Crying, even if prolonged as long as eight days, is considered a normal part of weaning, and few women consider weaning a difficult problem. The child does receive more attention during this period, however, sometimes going to live with the grandmother for a few days. Occasionally, if a child is inconsolable, he may be spanked or frightened into silence by being told that a coyote will come to eat him.

Illness and even death are frequent in children just after weaning. The change in diet may cause indigestion, diarrhea, or malnutrition. After weaning or the birth of another sibling, the close ties between the mother and the youngest child are broken. The child no longer sleeps with his mother, is not treated with the same indulgence and tenderness, is not kept as clean, and is given over to the care of older brothers and sisters.

Children between the ages of two and five are usually kept at home. They play with their brothers and sisters, cousins, or close neighbors in the patio and *corral* and are not permitted to go into the street unaccompanied by a grownup. They may join the games of the older children and learn many customs by playing house, school, *compadres,* fiesta, baptism, musician, funeral, and other games imitating adult behavior. Small children may receive rough treatment during play, either intentionally or unintentionally, and may be frightened or bribed into silence by the older ones. When young children are taken by their mother to the plaza or on a visit, they often show great timidity. Such nervous habits as chewing on clothing begin at this time. Enuresis is very common up to the age of five and is not infrequent in boys and girls of seven. It is not considered much of a problem, although children are scolded and shamed for it. Masturbation is not tolerated and is swiftly punished. Curiosity about the body and its functions is not encouraged. The questions we asked about the sex play of children received a blanket denial from parents, who maintained that their children were innocent and knew nothing of life. But from the life stories we gathered, it was clear that sex play does occur secretively and in games.

As children grow older they are put under more pressure to be obedient in preparation for their future work. At about five they are given such small chores as carrying corn in a little can when going with the mother or older sister to the mill, borrowing things from a neighbor or a relative, feeding the chickens, or taking care of a younger sibling. Boys of five often have the regular daily chore of carrying a few small cans of water from the fountain and of bringing in firewood or charcoal from the patio. Girls are expected to settle down to regular work sooner than boys and are more apt to be punished for carelessness or laziness.

Children of School Age

Beginning school is the next important step in the life of a Tepoztecan child. Children of from four to six are accepted in kindergarten, but many parents are reluctant to send their children so early because they fear for their physical safety and because they believe that too early learning will "heat their heads." Most children therefore begin in the first grade between the ages of seven and nine. In any one year, school enrollment is highest in the first and second grades, lower in kindergarten, and successively lower in the third, fourth, fifth, and sixth grades. In 1941, approximately 49 percent of the children between the ages of six and fifteen were enrolled in school; throughout the six grades the enrollment of girls was consistently lower than that of boys.

According to the teaching staff of the central school, the most serious school problem is nonattendance. Absence from school is extremely high during all important fiestas and when work is heavy in the fields. Tardiness is also a problem because most parents are not time conscious and may keep a child home until he has completed his chores. Only a minority of the parents give school attendance priority over work. The ability to read and write on a simple level satisfies the standards of most mothers and fathers.

Fearfulness and crying among the children are problems in the kindergarten and the first grade. These children are sometimes too timid to ask to be taken to the toilet, and the results may be unfortunate. A first-grade teacher reported that children who had attended kindergarten showed much less fear than children who entered the first grade without previous schooling. Apparently the socializing role of the school in Tepoztlán is important. Second-grade children are more self-confident and mischievous; third- and fourth-grade children tend to be less respectful and more disobedient. Boys in these grades frequently play truant. Fifth- and sixth-grade pupils are the most serious and studious.

The influence of the school has been profound, not only for the children but for the village as a whole. Although schools have existed in Tepoztlán for about a century, they formerly affected only a small percentage of the better-to-do families. Now the school teaches most Tepoztecan children new ways of living as well as the usual academic skills. New standards of personal hygiene, diet, dress, social participation, public health, and family relationships are taught. The celebration of Mother's Day, Children's Day, and secular and patriotic national holidays is encouraged. New games learned in the school emphasize teamwork, competition, scoring, definite goals, loyalty, leadership, sportsmanship, and physical exercise. In contrast, the traditional games were characterized by quiet play, little or no physical skill or exertion, and little competition.

Going to school does not have the same significance for girls as for boys. To girls who were traditionally confined to the home, burdened with household chores, and permitted little leisure, school represents freedom and pleasurable activity. To be relieved of work and close surveillance for six hours a day and to be able to play with children of the same age and to form friendships with both girls and boys are the most valued advantages the school offers to girls. They tend to feel deprived if they have to leave school. On the other hand boys, who traditionally had more freedom than their sisters, associate school with confinement. Most boys prefer to tend animals, work in the fields, or play truant.

The school has not only helped reduce the amount of work done by children but for many it has also postponed the age at which they contribute to their own support. It has in fact disrupted the traditional division of labor and has thrown a heavier burden of work on the parents. Going to school has in addition awakened new desires in children by removing them from the limited sphere of parental influence. They are no longer content to stay within patio walls at the beck and call of their mother; they urgently want to be with friends and to play after school. Play always has been, and still is, considered a possible source of danger and a waste of time by parents. A constant tug of war now goes on between parents and children as to how much time should be given to play.

Rorschach tests given in 1943 to thirty-nine children of school age revealed that the strongest formative influences were still the traditional, familiar ones. For fourteen younger children (ages five to eight) little difference between the sexes was found. A few of the children were quite responsive and showed spontaneity and interest in the world around them. Apparently they were being allowed to enjoy themselves. Furthermore, they seemed to be accepted by adults in a matter-of-fact, detached manner. The tests of twenty-five older children (ages nine to twelve) showed clear-cut sex differences. The girls seemed to be expected to act like adults and were being pushed beyond their years, but they showed no signs of revolt or worry and were in control of their impulses. The boys had a somewhat broader interest in everyday events, exhibited more spontaneity, and did not seem to be forced to have interests beyond their years. Both boys and girls in the older group seemed to live in a less warm and accepting environment than the younger children. They also showed little creative fantasy and did not allow themselves freedom for enjoyment.

Adolescence and Courtship

The period between childhood and adulthood is ill-defined and un-marked by special occasion or ceremony in Tepoztlán. This period has been extended by several years in recent times and has begun to have the charac-teristics of adolescence as we know it. Not long ago girls were called *niñas* (children) until twelve and *señoritas* until fourteen. Often they went directly from *niña* to *señora* because of early marriage. Now girls are called *niñas* until fifteen and *señoritas* until marriage. Most parents still make twelve the transition point, however, and withdraw their daughters from school and expect them to conduct themselves not as children but as *señoritas*.

Boys have not been hurried into adulthood by early marriage but they have been expected to assume full-time adult work by fifteen. At one time this age was ten. As compared with girls, the changes in age status for boys occur later, more gradually, and with less strain. Boys are called *muchachos* from about seven to eighteen or until they marry. Youths older than eighteen may also be called *jovenes* until marriage. No fixed or recommended age for mar-riage has been established for boys. Unmarried youths, however, are not en-trusted with positions of responsibility in the barrio nor may they hold public office.

Adolescents usually do not attend school but work for their parents. They thus become a decided economic asset to the family rather than a burden. The dependence of the parents on the children becomes clearer at this time and the young people tend to have a more secure position in the family. In contrast with our own society, there is a notable absence of open "revolt" against the authority and example of parents or of local tradition; the excep-tions occur in connection with courtship and elopement. The authoritarian family and the lack of alternatives have tended to produce young people who are passive and dependent. A very small percentage are willing or able to strike out on their own, and no pattern of running away from home "to seek one's fortune" exists in the village. The only evidences of some break with tradition are shown by a very small group of boys and girls who have studied outside the village. As we shall see later, these patterns are rapidly changing.

In terms of behavior and experience, the period of adolescence has, however, a different—almost a contrasting—significance for boys and for girls. For girls it brings additional personal restrictions, chaperonage, a larger burden of not entirely desirable work, and few rewards. Between twelve and fifteen, girls are expected to give up their friends and play habits and to devote themselves to household chores. They are given almost the entire care of younger siblings, though they have little authority over them. On a girl's fifteenth birthday her parents prepare her for marriage by giving her a pair of shoes to wear on holidays, a bright-colored dress and apron, and perhaps silver or gold earrings. From then on she pays a great deal of attention to her appearance and is usually better groomed than either *niñas* or married women. She must now do almost everything that a married woman does—wash and iron the larger pieces of clothing, sew, grind corn and coffee, make different types of tortillas, cook all the food eaten by the family, and learn to prepare complicated fiesta dishes.

The appearance of the first menses is a traumatic experience for most girls, since they have usually been kept in ignorance of it. They associate it with something shameful, dirty, and even punishable, and keep it secret. Girls who remain in school longer generally learn about it sooner and feel less fear and guilt, but many girls express some shame and disgust about it. In the past, when girls married before puberty, it was widely believed that menstruation was caused by sexual intercourse. This belief has still not been entirely eradicated. The grandmother or the mother eventually gives the girl advice on proper behavior during menstruation. They warn that bathing or washing the feet or eating "cold" foods such as pork, avocado, beans, and lemon might stop the flow. Menstruation is expected to last three days and the flow is generally sparse.

The adjustment of an adolescent girl to her home situation varies considerably. In large part it depends upon her relations with her mother. The close relationship between adolescent girl and mother is recent in Tepoztlán, for child marriage and patrilocal residence effectively severed the mother-daughter tie in past years. The young daughter-in-law was considered a main source of help to the mother-in-law, and many of the attitudes of the mother-in-law—daughter-in-law relationship were later carried over to the mother-daughter relationship. Mothers of grown daughters tend to "retire" from most of the heavy household duties and to assume the role of director rather than that of partner. The life stories we have gathered show that at least in retrospect women resent their mothers for having overworked them. On the whole, however, adolescent girls seem satisfied with the more rewarding aspects of their life—nicer clothes, little luxuries that their parents see fit to buy for them, trips to the plaza or the mill, and attendance at church and fiestas. Courtship provides a good deal of excitement although it is also a source of worry and fear.

For boys, adolescence brings greater freedom than before and more respectful treatment at home. They begin to work seriously at farming, the most important and best-rewarded work in the village. Most boys and youths enjoy farming and are pleased at the prospect of becoming a peasant. When a boy is able to do a man's work, his status improves noticeably; he is given a larger share of food, clothing, and spending money, is served equally with his father, and has more authority over younger siblings. The work relations between father and son are generally smoother than those between mother and daughter. The authoritarian, reserved figure of the father usually inspires complete obedience from the son. Moreover, fathers tend to be patient in teaching their sons, and the work is done side by side, with the father usually taking the heavier burden.

Adolescent interest in modern sports is becoming a source of conflict. Parents object to the playing of soccer, volleyball, and pool—the three most popular sports among boys—as childish, wasteful, and dangerous. They believe that sports use up the precious energy needed in the *milpas;* they say the ax, *machete,* and team of oxen provide all the exercise a farmer can endure. Mothers complain that the boys get overheated and then are particularly susceptible to *los aires.* Older men dislike the new sports because they are replacing the older diversions such as rodeos and cockfights.

The most important diversion for youths and one that gives them a real sense of achievement is courtship—a relatively new phenomenon in Tepoztlán. Before the Revolution, most marriages were arranged by the parents with or without the consent of the children. The engaged couple were not permitted to be alone together and sometimes were not even acquainted before marriage. Only betrothed couples from the few better-to-do, literate families courted secretly by exchanging love letters. Today courtship and the sending of love letters are common in the village, and few girls over thirteen or boys over fifteen do not have a sweetheart. The local priest has recognized this situation and has stated publicly that having a *novio* is not a sin and need not be mentioned in confession. A great deal of secrecy still surrounds courtship, however, and the girl still fears punishment.

As a first step in courting the boy sends the girl a letter declaring his love. Some boys may send several anonymous letters before they have the courage to sign their name. Boys with more education and self-confidence may initiate courtship in person by trying to detain the girl on the street. If the girl consents to let him walk by her side, he will at once propose that they be *novios.* It is a common sight to see a young boy loitering around a street corner for hours, waiting to get a glimpse of his *novia* or to say a few words to her. This "cornering" of a girl is a regular courting practice in Tepoztlán. At night boys often gather at a corner to play the guitar and serenade a nearby *novia* of one of the group.

Because of the difficulty in meeting, sending letters is a necessity after a boy and girl become *novios.* Letters may be left in a secret place or delivered by a trusted friend or a child. Widows and girls may be hired for the purpose of delivering love messages, patching quarrels, or convincing a girl to become someone's *novia.* Known by the insulting terms of *alcahuetes* or *corre-ve-y-dile* (run-see-and-tell), such go-betweens are strongly disapproved of; they are also suspected of knowing how to use sorcery particularly appropriate for *novios.* Love magic may be resorted to if courting is difficult. Powdered bone from a human skull, placed in a girl's hand, in her hair, or in a sweet drink, will make her fall in love. The leg of a beetle placed in a girl's drink will make her desire sexual relations. The use of sorcery for revenge by a jilted *novia* is very much feared by young men. The *novia* is believed to be able to make her former lover ill by sticking pins through a picture of him. Chronic illness in young men is often attributed to some girl's black magic.

Novios do not necessarily marry and may or may not have sexual relations. They generally caress and embrace but rarely kiss. Kissing is a modern innovation of courtship which only the more sophisticated have adopted. It is common today to have several *novios* before marriage, but a girl who has many *novios,* or who has them simultaneously, is called *loca* or crazy and severely criticized. A boy who has many *novias* is credited with being *macho* or manly but is not considered a desirable marriage partner.

Rorschach responses of twenty-five girls and boys between the ages of thirteen and nineteen clearly reflect the different training and experience of the two sexes. The girls seem to be under more control; apparently they are expected to refrain from sexual activity and to carry out their duties. They have low energy drives, are less responsive than the boys and suppress their fantasies and impulses. They follow the pattern of older women; they are detached from childish interests and are most impressed by the concrete, everyday aspects of their life. Like the girls of from nine to twelve years, these girls seem to have been pushed into an adult female pattern, but they do not seem to be enjoying it.

In contrast, the boys are more expansive in their contacts with the world about them, have more varied experiences and interests, and exhibit less control over their fantasies and feelings. They are interested in the opposite sex and are trying hard to act like men; at the same time, they show some anxiety about their sexual fantasies and activities.

Marriage

Marriage is important in establishing adult status. Men who are married and are heads of families hold positions of leadership and are responsible for local government and politics. Women move to a higher status when they become mothers. There are three types of marriage in Tepoztlán: civil marriage, church marriage, and free union. In 1940, one-half of all the marriages in the village were both civil and church law, one-fourth were church only, 15 percent were free unions, and 10 percent were civil law alone. Civil marriage has been required by law since 1928; before that, most formal marriages were church law only. Church marriage still carries the greatest prestige, but the number of civil marriages is now steadily increasing although their status is almost as low status as that of free unions.

Most girls marry between the ages of fifteen and seventeen and most boys between nineteen and twenty. If a girl is not married by the time she is twenty, she is considered an old maid who will "dress saints" for the rest of her life. More and more girls are delaying marriage, however, to go through secondary school and become teachers. As noted earlier, the great majority of Tepoztecans marry within their own village. In 1944, only 10 percent of the marriages involved outsiders and even then the nonvillage partner came either from other villages of the municipio or from nearby regions. Almost one-half of the marriages are between members of the same *barrio* within the village. Patrilocal residence is the rule although a good number of matrilocal arrangements occur.

Romantic reasons—a girl's beauty or personality—are usually behind a boy's selection of a wife. Girls are more concerned with finding a husband who does not drink, chase women, or have the reputation of being aggressive.

Status factors are important for both sexes. Boys prefer a girl who is poorer than they and who has less education so that "the man can be the boss." They tend to "respect" and to avoid having affairs with the daughters of the more prosperous families for fear of incurring reprisals. Girls, on the other hand, try to improve their economic status with marriage, and it is rare for a girl to marry a man with less education. As a result, the daughters of the better-to-do families have difficulty finding husbands and tend to marry later or to marry men from outside the village.

In giving their blessing to a marriage, parents are chiefly concerned with the practical considerations of the prospective mate's health and his family's reputation. They are interested in the personal qualities of a daughter-in-law more than of a son-in-law, although laziness, drunkenness, disobedience, or rebelliousness in the latter would cause them to oppose the marriage. The traditional, most respectable form of arranging a marriage is the *petición de mano,* or asking for the girl's hand. This is done by the boy's father and by his godfather of baptism. The mother may act as a substitute or, if the boy is an orphan, an uncle, or the godfather alone. Formerly, the parents chose a wife for their son and asked for his approval. Now the procedure is reversed; usually the boy and girl have secretly become *novios* and agree to the marriage beforehand. When the *petición de mano* occurs, the girl's parents ask for a stay of a few weeks as a matter of form. A request for a stay of one year is tantamount to a refusal. When the decision is favorable, the girl's parents question the boy about his willingness to undertake the obligation of supporting a wife. They warn him of their daughter's faults to prevent him from being dissatisfied with her after marriage and blaming them. They also give advice to their daughter: she must try to please her husband and his parents, work hard, be obedient, avoid being jealous, and not leave the house without her husband's permission. If these conversations are satisfactory, a date for the wedding is set.

In the past, an underlying idea of marriage arrangements was to compensate the bride's family for the loss of a working member. A formal bride price, known as the *chichitomin,* which means payment for the mother's milk with which the girl was raised, was paid by the groom's family. It was paid in silver pesos and varied from a few pesos to twenty-five or thirty. In addition, the young man was expected to bring wood and water to his future in-laws for a period of one or two years, and the boy's mother brought flowers and candles in the name of the girl's saint every eight days for a month before the marriage. The boy's parents also brought gifts of chocolate, bread, and wine every Sunday from the time of the *petición de mano* until the wedding day. These practices are no longer followed. The boy's mother, however, is still expected to bring gifts during the marriage negotiations.

If there is opposition to the marriage from either set of parents, the couple usually elopes. Elopements in Tepoztlán do not have the same romantic connotations they have in the United States. Rather they result from the negativism of the parents, the fear and rebellion of the daughter, the assertion of the boy over his *novia,* the wish to escape wedding expenses, or, at worst, the absence of a sense of responsibility on the part of the youth. When an elopement or *rapto* occurs, the couple go to live as man and wife in the home of a well-disposed aunt or uncle or friend. If the boy intends to marry, his parents formally ask the girl's parents for her hand. If either set of parents remains intransigent, the couple may never marry or at least not in church. Most parents accept an elopement as a *fait accompli,* however, and marriage follows. The practice of elopement is old in Tepoztlán but it has increased considerably since the Revolution. In 1942-43, approximately 50 percent of all marriages began as elopements.

To be well married in Tepoztlán is to be married in church. In order to provide a fine church wedding, a boy's parents may sell their animals or pawn their house or, if they are unwilling to do this, the boy may work outside the home and save his money for the wedding. Church weddings are becoming increasingly expensive, the cost ranging from 300 to 1,000 pesos. A wedding in the church follows Catholic tradition with local variations. On the evening before the wedding, the boy's parents send a basket of bread, chocolate, wine, and turkey to the girl's home as well as the white wedding dress with its train and veil, shoes, stockings, and flowers. The girl and the clothes are taken to the home of the godparents of marriage, where the girl spends the night. The godparents give her marital advice, emphasizing the fact that she must obey her husband. In the early morning the godmother helps her wash and dress and the godfather delivers the bride to the groom at the church door. The marriage vows, the placing of the ring, and the giving of the thirteen coins (*arrastomines*) take place at the church door, after which the couple enter the church for the Mass.

After the ceremony the wedding party returns to the godparents' home where refreshments are served and where the couple again receive marital advice. At noon the couple and their guests go to the groom's house. Some couples still carry burning incense over the threshold, but this custom is disappearing. A festive dinner of *mole poblano* follows. From then on for a year or two the couple live in the groom's house, in many cases sleeping in the same room with the rest of the family.

Civil marriage is much simpler and less expensive, and partly for this reason it is increasing. If a couple decide to live in free union, there is no celebration or announcement of any kind. The more acculturated Tepoztecans no longer regard free union as a form of marriage, no matter how many years a couple live together nor how many children they have. Most villagers, however, regard such a couple as man and wife and their children as having equal rights with other children. About a half of the free unions involve young people, although for most of them it is a second marriage.

Rorschach tests given to twenty-one adults between the ages of twenty and thirty-nine show that the young married Tepoztecan woman has learned to conform and to accept her role in life without asking for sympathy or understanding. She is a controlled, efficient individual who takes care of the material needs of everyday living with less tension than the adolescent girl. But she shows few signs of liveliness or warmth, expresses no emotional needs, and does not offer love and affection. She seems to receive little satisfaction from sex, is passive and adaptive, timid and cautious, and accepting of male domination.

On the basis of the test protocols, the young adult male seems to be fairly secure in his role as master of the house and capable of making decisions and maintaining authority. There are evidences of a carry-over of the anxiety concerning sex that was seen in the adolescent boy, however; probably the adult male is able to function well only when he feels secure in his sexual role. Indications of impulsivity, depression, and bodily preoccupation are apparent also, but these are under control.

Old Age and Death

Traditionally, old age is the time when a Tepoztecan receives the greatest respect and consideration; the consensus, however, is that less and less respect is now being shown to old people. Children have begun to address their grandparents in the familiar *tu* and some of the old customs of respect—kissing the hand of older people, for example—are falling into disuse. Old men no longer take part in politics and do not generally have positions of leadership. Because the culture is changing rapidly, the *ancianos* find themselves out of step with the times. Their values conflict with those of the younger generation, and, moreover, some of them speak Spanish poorly. They are treated with relative respect, however, and the grandparent-grandchild relationship is often a very affectionate one.

It is not old age as such that is feared by Tepoztecans, but dependence on others, or the inability to be self-supporting. Most old people work until they can no longer stand. The situation of the aged varies considerably from family to family. Ownership of property, particularly the kind that brings in a cash income from rental, is the best assurance for a secure old age, and for this reason parents usually do not divide their property among the children before their death. But most of the people in the village are poor, owning only their house and site and perhaps a few fruit trees and a pig; they can be self-supporting only by working. Many old women, especially widows, take in washing and ironing, raise pigs and chickens, sell tortillas, fruit, and produce, or earn money as midwives and *curanderas*. There are few nonstrenuous jobs for old men who can no longer farm. The lack of handicraft skills or other means of support is a real handicap to these men.

The Rorschach records of twenty-one men and women between the ages of forty-seven and seventy-four show a marked contrast with the records of young adults. The control and discipline learned by women in their younger years become their strength in old age. Undisturbed by daydreams, sexual urges, and emotional needs, the older woman takes over the household and becomes its dominant member. She still functions in a concrete, realistic way, but she is rigid, pedantic, and fussy. She is also efficient and determined. She still does not show warmth toward people, however, or the desire to cooperate in a friendly way. Older men, in contrast, have moved from a conventional, everyday way of life to a more uncontrolled and explosively emotional one. They seem to be unreflective, given to impulsive outbursts, thoughts, and ideas. They show some preoccupation with sexual functioning and have feelings of impotence. It is as though they are overwhelmed by circumstances they cannot handle and react with impulsivity, anxiety, depression, and helplessness. Apparently they have lost the mastery of their world and are traumatized and conflicted by it.

Death apparently inspires no undue fear or preoccupation. Old people freely speak of death, using the expressions, "when I am dead," or "when I am underground." Perhaps because from childhood Tepoztecans have not been protected from the facts of death, they see it as a natural occurrence. Display of grief is restrained at a death, although it varies according to the age and status of the deceased. Suicide is uncommon, and in no case has anyone killed himself because of the death of a loved one. When a Tepoztecan dies soon after the death of someone close to him, however, it is often said that he died of *sentimiento* or grief. The death of an old person or of an infant causes relatively little emotional disturbance.

Tepoztecans are concerned with the release of the soul from the body at death and with its journey to heaven. They say that those who have led wicked lives have difficulty giving up their souls and take a long time to die. They say also that often children "cannot die until they receive a benediction from their parents or godparents" and that a father or a mother "cannot die if their children cry too much." In such cases the children are taken away to hasten the death. When death comes, the soul leaves the body and may be seen as a white, foamlike figure which resembles the deceased and which walks without touching the ground but disappears after leaving the house.

When a person is at the point of death, he is taken from his bed and placed on a *petate* on the floor. With death the body is dressed with clean clothes, covered with a sheet, and placed on a table. A newspaper is spread on the *petate* and a cross of sand and lime is fashioned on the paper. Flowers are placed above the cross, and a candle, kept burning day and night for nine days, is placed at the head of the *petate*. If the deceased is a man, his sombrero and huaraches are laid next to the candle; if a woman, her *rebozo*. All the clothes of the dead person are washed and ironed and also laid on the *petate*. A *rezandero* is hired by the bereaved family to come to the house to pray twice a day for nine days. The women of the house are required to be present on these occasions and to kneel in prayer. A wake is held day and night, and coffee, alcohol, bread, and cigarettes are provided for those who come to keep vigil. Close relatives may help with the expenses. At the death of a young godchild, most godparents fulfill their obligations to provide a coffin, burial clothing, and perhaps music.

The next day a few men go to the cemetery to dig the grave. The deceased is placed in a coffin and, accompanied by the mourners, is carried to the cemetery. If the deceased is a prominent person or a member of the *Acción Católica,* the funeral procession may enter the church for a benediction before proceeding to the burial place. The church bells will be rung if a special fee is paid. On the ninth day or *novena* the ceremony of the raising of the cross of lime and sand takes place at a night wake similar to the one held on the day of the death. This time, however, an offering of tamales, *mole verde,* oranges, chocolate, and bread is left for twelve hours on the altar in the home in order to provide the deceased with food for each month of the year.

For the raising of the cross, a boy and girl who are not relatives are selected to act as *padrinos.* Accompanied by the *rezandero* and carrying flowers, the two children walk toward the *petate* which holds the cross of lime and sand. Prayers are first recited and the children are then given new brooms with which they sweep the sand and lime onto a tray that is later carried to the grave. The clothes of the deceased are also raised. As each article is picked up, the *padrinos* recite a prayer. The ceremony closes with the singing of hymns in honor of the dead. A year after the death another wake may be held, a special Mass arranged and the grave revisited.

A child's funeral is somewhat different. Because the child's soul goes directly to heaven, it is supposed to be a joyous occasion, and gay music is played. The child is dressed like San Jose if a boy, like the Virgin of Guadalupe if a girl. A crown of paper flowers is placed on the head, the face covered with a veil, and the feet fitted into socks and sandals lined with gold paper. When the body is laid out, the hands and feet are tied together with ribbons, which are untied at the grave. A small painted gourd, placed beside the body, is believed to provide the soul with water during its journey to heaven. The litter is carried by children of the same sex as the deceased and, as the body is taken out of the house, the barrio chapel bell is rung.

7

Ethos

THE TRADITIONAL world-view of Tepoztecans has been conditioned by the limitations of their physical environment, technology, and economy, by their turbulent history, by their three-hundred years of colonial status, by their poverty and high death rate, and finally by the haphazard nature of social changes caused by urban influences. To Tepoztecans, the world and nature present a constant threat of calamity and danger. A strong fear of natural forces and a high anxiety about the imminence of misfortune, disaster, and death were revealed in Thematic Apperception Test stories and in dreams collected from a sample of the villagers. The sample included members of the younger generation who had been under the influence of the school.

The world in which Tepoztecans live is filled with hostile forces and punishing figures which must be propitiated if their good will and protection are to be secured. El Tepozteco withholds rain if he is neglected; *los aires,* the spirits who live in the water, send illness to those who offend them; and *naguales,* humans in pact with the devil, can turn themselves into a pig or dog to do harm at night. Catholic figures, too, are seen as threatening. God is a punishing figure rather than one of love, and most misfortunes are ascribed to Him. He brings good fortune only rarely.

The saints are seen as intermediaries between God and man, and Tepoztecans devote themselves to cultivating their favor. The saints with the greater punishing power—for example, Saint Peter of the barrio of San Pedro—are the most assiduously worshiped. If not enough dancers turn out for Saint Peter's feast day, he brings illness and bad luck to those who did not participate. He is also said to use the lion, whose image accompanies his, to frighten children into dancing for him. The lion will also be sent to frighten a villager who does not accept the office of *mayordomo* of the barrio of San Pedro.

Most Tepoztecans do not distinguish clearly between the punishments of God and the work of *el pingo,* the devil. The powers of the devil are relatively few, however, and may be mitigated by reciting a prayer to Saint Michael or to Saint Gabriel. (To avoid angering the devil, a small candle is lighted to him at the same time.) Nor do Tepoztecans have a clear conception of the Catholic heaven and hell. The Aztec religion depicted heaven as a pleasant place reserved for dead warriors and women who died in childbirth. The equivalent of hell was only a region of the dead, *Mictlan,* where souls continued to live the same life as they had on earth. Hell as a place for expiating sins committed in life was totally unknown, and many Tepoztecans still have no notion of eternal punishment. Hell is thought, rather, to be a purgatory which punishes only the greatest sinners. Ordinary people do not fear hell and usually have no concern with sin, with confession, or with life after death.

The profoundly practical nature of Tepoztecans precludes religious fantasy, mysticism, or any preoccupation with metaphysics. They seek from religion concrete solutions to the problems of daily life. They can understand punishment for things done or not done and the need for protection. They bow to superior powers by doing what is expected of them or by giving or doing something that should please a particular being: lighting a candle, offering a few coins or flowers, burning incense, reciting a special prayer, or performing a certain dance. They believe these offerings incur an obligation on the part of the recipient to favor or protect the donor.

To traditional Catholic symbols Tepoztecans impart magical powers which give them additional protection. They receive the Ash on Ash Wednesday in the belief that the cross, the formal Catholic symbol of penance and sorrow, will guard them against sorcery and enemies. Old holy images are burned to make more efficacious ashes. The palm blessed on Palm Sunday is used for protection against lightning; its ashes are used to cure headaches. Peasants trim their plants on Holy Saturday so that they will produce more, mothers cut their daughters' hair to make it grow longer, and children are struck on the legs to make them taller. On September 28, crosses of *pericón* that have been pressed are placed on doorways and *milpas* to ward off demons and evil winds.

Tepoztecans view people, too, as potentially hostile and dangerous, and their typical reaction is a defensive one. Security in the threatening world is sought first and foremost through the economic independence of the biological family. To be able to provide one's wife and children with food, clothing, and shelter is the only real assurance against want and interference. Work, industry, and thrift, for the purpose of accumulating property in land and animals, are the highest, most enduring values in Tepoztlán. So long as a man devotes himself to work, he feels secure and blameless, regardless of how little he produces. Material success is not openly admitted as an important personal goal and is not admired in others. With faith in his own power and with the help of God, the Tepoztecan lives as an individualist, withdrawn, self-reliant, reluctant to seek or give economic aid, or to borrow or lend. Despite the tradition of collective labor, there is a general unwillingness to cooperate with others in public and private enterprises.

The Tepoztecan's individualism and independence are tempered, how-ever, by his loyalty to and cooperation with his immediate family. The de-pendence of families on the communal lands and the occasional need for group effort to defend these lands and to maintain public property also modify Tepoztecan individualism. This individualism, however, is not competitive as in the United States. In the village, the individual does not try to win security and recognition through development of his personal talents or through self-aggrandizement but rather through conformity and submission to the needs of his family. It is an enclosing, inward-turning individualism which permits fami-lies to live side by side in privacy and with no power over one another. This is what gives the village its segmentalized character.

Tepoztecans also seek security through respect and the extension of the respect relationship, which they value highly as a safe one. In such a relation-ship each party is guaranteed friendly, respectful behavior and the fulfillment of formal obligations. Respect status may stem from a superior social, eco-nomic, or political position, from advanced age, from education, or from a specific, formal relationship established between two individuals or families— for example, in-laws or *compadres*. Among young people who have studied outside the village there is now a tendency toward the urban usage of *tu* and *Usted;* this means the practice of using *tu* only for relatives and intimate friends and using *Usted* for all others. This results in fewer *tu* and more *Usted* relationships.

Tepoztecans are not an easy people to get to know, for they are not outgoing or expressive. Most interpersonal relationships are characterized by reserve and carefully guarded behavior. The man who speaks little, minds his own business, and maintains some distance between himself and others is considered prudent and wise. The people are sombre and quiet, especially in the street. Boisterousness and noise coming from a house soon earns the family an unpleasant reputation. Women and girls are expected to walk with eyes modestly downcast; those who smile freely may be thought flirtatious or flippant. To smile very much at other peoples' babies is to be suspected of the evil eye. Most children do not learn to smile at strangers or visitors until they attend school. Tepoztecan men, particularly, tend to be undemonstrative and limited in their ability to express warmth and affection and the more tender emotions. One informant succinctly described himself and his fellow villagers by saying, *"Somos muy secos"*—that is, "We are very dry."

Creativity and artistic expression are limited to the point of constriction. As noted earlier, there are practically no handicrafts, no pottery, woodcarving, weaving, or basketmaking. Music and dancing are not well developed. Reli-gious artistic expression consists only of decorating the church at fiestas and of making costumes and masks for a few annual religious dances. Clay utensils and household articles are for the most part undecorated. The clothes of the village women are traditionally drab, although young girls are now beginning to wear brighter colored dresses. Bright colors, particularly in clothing, have not been in accord with Tepoztecan ideas of propriety and in the past were actually believed to be dangerous because they might attract the rainbow. Most of the color in Tepoztlán comes from the beautiful flowers that grow in the gardens.

Constriction is also evidenced in Tepoztecans' gestures and in their avoidance of bodily contact with others. Perhaps the only major exception occurs in the mother-child relationship during the nursing period; after a child is five, he experiences little physical contact of a tender nature. Kissing, except of infants, is not customary even in courtship, as we have seen. From the Spanish, Tepoztecans learned the gesture of kissing the hand of the priest, parents, grandparents, and godparents but this custom is now disappearing. Shaking hands and the typical Mexican double embrace are not generally practiced in Tepoztlán. It is when Tepoztecans drink that their restraint relaxes; male companions may then walk arm-in-arm and, as we mentioned earlier, drunken men sometimes try to hug and even kiss their children or wives.

Normally, the Tepoztecan shows his affection for another by fulfilling reciprocal obligations: the father expresses love for his wife and children by providing them with the necessities of life; the child shows affection by obedience, respect, and diligence; *compadres* and members of the extended family demonstrate their friendship and goodwill by carrying out their formal duties. When these obligations are carried out, Tepoztecans consider that they have a satisfactory relationship with each other and demand little more. Some of the younger people, it is true, are no longer content with formal reciprocity and seek out friends on the basis of personal interest. Younger parents are beginning to express affection for their children through gift giving and through greater indulgence and concern with their children's aspirations.

Tepoztecans place value on sexual restraint not because they are puritanical or guilt ridden but because of practical considerations of safety and self-preservation. They believe in conserving themselves for work. They also fear too strong attachments, unwanted pregnancies, and jealousy and sorcery. From childhood on, sexuality is discouraged and discussion of sex is taboo in the home; infant sexuality, masturbation, and sex play among children are strictly forbidden. For women, there is little inconsistency between childhood training and acceptable adult behavior. Girls grow up with negative, prudish attitudes toward sex, marriage, and childbearing; they are expected to be sexually restrained both before and after marriage. For males, however, a discontinuity exists in connection with sex. Although sexuality is inhibited all through childhood, young men are subjected to pressure from members of their age group to be sexually active; they are expected to prove their manliness through sexual conquests both before and after marriage. In practice, however, the attitudes toward sex and the slow development of boys create an aura of anxiety about sexual activity and boys are often timid in courtship. The prevailing attitude is, nevertheless, that sexual activity in men is an expression of manliness, while in women it is a form of delinquency.

Tepoztecans are an indirect people who rely on formality and intermediaries to facilitate interpersonal relations. Any direct expression of aggression is discouraged and competition between individuals is rare. Underlying the smooth surface, however, is a feeling of oppression, particularly for those individuals who are trying to improve themselves or who, for one reason or another, deviate from strict conformity. A good deal of suppressed hostility finds indirect release in malicious gossip, stealing, secret destruction of other's property, envy, deprecation, and sorcery. The *indirecta* or indirect criticism is a common, accepted form of aggression. Assault in the form of surprise attack and murder occurs from time to time. Men in positions of wealth, power, or authority often carry a gun for protection and prefer not to venture out at night. The most feared, although perhaps the least common, form of indirect aggression is sorcery.

The sanctions against any overt expression of aggression sometimes give rise to an interesting type of illness known as *muina* or anger, in which the aggression is apparently turned inward against the self. The symptoms of *muina* are loss of appetite, inability to keep down food, loss of weight, and very often death. *Muina* is a fairly common condition and occurs among members of both sexes; it is mainly an adult illness but children sometimes have it. It may be caused by insults, humiliation, bad luck, or any frustration that arouses anger.

In Tepoztlán the motives of everyone are suspect, from the highest public officials of the nation to the local priest and even close relatives. It is assumed that anyone who has power will use it to his own advantage. Honest government or leadership is considered an impossibility; altruism is not understood. The frank, direct person, if he exists anywhere in the village, is thought to be naive or the greatest rogue of all, so powerful or so shameless as to have no need to conceal his actions or thoughts. Friendships are few. To have friendships outside the extended family is not a Tepoztecan ideal, nor is there a long tradition of a "best friend." Adults consider friends a source of trouble and a waste of time. Traditionally, women and girls are not supposed to have any friends whatsoever. While men may be friendly with many individuals, these relations tend to be based on a definite, limited purpose—that is, for work exchange, or for borrowing, or for drinking together.

There is a relative lack of concern for the future, and no "saving for a rainy day." Only a minority who recognize education as an important source of security save for an advanced education for a son or daughter. And it is only among these families that one encounters the familiar urban middle-class pattern of self-denial in the present in order to gain a future reward. The rest of the villagers exercise a general thrift, but they spend when they have money and pull in their belts when they have none. Young people planning to be married do not save in anticipation of future needs but marry at short notice. As we have noted, the boy's parents supply the money for the wedding by selling an animal or by borrowing, and the boy sometimes goes to work for two or three months to raise the money.

The majority of Tepoztecans seem to lack strong drive or ambition for self-improvement. They tend to be satisfied if they have enough food and clothing from harvest to harvest. Among the young people, too, there is a general acceptance of the way of life. Young men wish to be peasants like their fathers and most young girls continue to work at home and to serve their elders. The rewards they seek are not impossible to achieve: occasional new clothes, shoes, a sweetheart, permission to attend the fiestas, and ultimately marriage, with some parental help.

Of particular interest for the understanding of the relative absence of frustration, anxiety, guilt, and self-blame is the tendency to shift personal responsibility onto others or onto impersonal forces and to explain noncon- formity in terms of magical or other supernatural forces. The individual cannot help what he does, for these forces control him. Such traits as fatalism, stoicism in the face of misfortune, passivity, acceptance of things as they are, and a general readiness to expect the worst tend to free the individual from the bur- den of being in control of his personal fate. Even in the face of gross injustice, in which a villager could be protected by law, there may be little or no self-defense.

The patterns of child training, which we have discussed earlier, reflect many adult attitudes and value systems. One of the underlying principles in child rearing is to develop children who are easy to control. The great amount of attention given an infant is primarily for the purpose of limiting and pro- tecting him rather than of stimulating him. Activity, aggression, self-gratifica- tion, curiosity, and independence are all discouraged from infancy through young adulthood. Although the young child, especially if he is a boy, is in- dulged in some ways and permitted a degree of ego development, so long as a son or daughter lives under the parental roof, he is dependent on the parents and subject to their authority—and this situation may continue through marriage.

Although, by and large, the training the child receives adequately pre- pares him for adult life in the village, nevertheless there are some points of conflict and inconsistency between theory and practice. Perhaps the primary area of conflict is found in the roles of men and women and in the relations between the sexes. On the whole, men are under greater pressure than women, experience more discontinuity in the transition from childhood to adulthood, and face greater contradictions between their ideal and actual social roles. Although boys are favored more than girls, their early training is not conducive to the development of independence or a real ability to dominate, qualities required by the ideals of a patriarchal society. We have seen that husbands frequently rely on fear to maintain authority. As the men grow older and as their sexual powers and their ability to work decline, they find it more difficult to keep their position of dominance; older men in the community receive little social recognition and have little power. It is interesting to note that the life cycles of men and women take an opposite course: in early life men are in a comparatively favored position but as they grow older they are weighed down by life situations. Women begin with less freedom, lower aspiration levels, and earlier responsibilities, but as they mature after marriage they slowly gain more freedom and often take a dominant position in the household.

Discrepancy between theory and practice in Tepoztecan society is also found in the different degree of socialization of men and women. The men have greater freedom and higher social status, but it is the women who seem to be better socialized. This greater socialization begins early in life. While girls are taking care of their brothers and sisters under the watchful eye of their mother, their brothers are out in the fields, often alone, guarding the animals. Women are seldom alone. At home they are surrounded by members of the family and have opportunities to chat with neighbors and relatives. Their daily trips to the plaza offer occasions for gossip and news. They attend church more often and prepare festive meals with the aid of other women. Men continue to spend most of their days alone at work in the fields. Occasions for communal work are few and even these seem to have to be accompanied by drinking. In fact, the men do not seem to be at ease in groups unless they are fortified by alcohol.

A highly respected native curer.

8

The Changing Village

T HE DESCRIPTION of Tepoztlán given in the preceding pages is based
largely on my study of the village in 1943. Since that time many changes
have occurred both in the village and in Mexico as a whole. Here I
will sketch briefly some of the major changes on the national level and then
examine those in the village as revealed by my restudy in 1956. In this way the
reader can see to what extent Tepoztlán has participated in national trends.

The Nation

Mexico has undergone great changes since 1940. The population has
increased by over ten million to reach a high of about thirty million in 1956.
This increase has been accompanied by a surge of urbanization, with millions
of peasants and villagers moving into the cities. The population growth of
Mexico City has been phenomenal—from one and a half million in 1940 to
four million in 1956. The economy has been expanding and the country has
become acutely production conscious. A boom spirit has been created reminiscent of the great expansion in the United States at the turn of the century.
Many Mexicans believe that their country has found a formula which will soon
take it out of the ranks of the underdeveloped nations and will serve as a
model to other countries.

Achievements in agriculture and industry have been record breaking;
in view of the arid nature of the country, those in agriculture are even more
impressive than those in industry. Since 1940, about a million and a half hectares have been brought under irrigation; the total harvested area has been
increased by about 70 percent; and the number of tractors has increased from
4,600 to over 55,000.

Increased national wealth has led to some improvement in the standard
of living of the general population. More and more rural people sleep on beds

instead of on the ground, wear shoes instead of huaraches or instead of going barefoot, use store-made pants instead of the home-made white *calzones,* eat bread in addition to tortillas, grind their corn in the mill instead of by hand, drink beer instead of pulque, use doctors instead of *curanderos,* and travel by bus or train instead of on foot and on burro. In the towns and cities the trend has been from adobe to cement, from clay pots to aluminum, from charcoal to gas cooking, from tortillas as eating "implements" to tableware, from the *metate* to the electric blender, from phonographs to radios and television, from cotton to nylon, and from cognac to whiskey.

Another significant trend since 1940 has been the increasing influence of United States culture. The major television programs are sponsored by foreign controlled companies and only the use of the Spanish language and Mexican artists distinguish some of the commercials from those in the United States. Such American department store retail practices as self-service, attractive open displays of goods, standardized and guaranteed articles, and fixed prices have been made more popular in the past ten years by stores like Woolworths and Sears and Roebuck. Self-service supermarkets, complete with packaged foods and many with American brands, are opening in the better-to-do neighborhoods of Mexico City and in some of the smaller towns. American-made clothing and shoes are sold in the higher priced shops.

Increased employment in factories and office buildings has led to the spread of the quick lunch, eliminating the midday meal at home as well as the traditional siesta. The American-style breakfast—juice, cereal, ham and eggs, and coffee—has become popular, displacing the traditional beans, chili sauce, and tortillas. The practice of eating roast turkey on Christmas eve has been adopted by some urban middle-class families. The same trend is seen in the substitution of the Christmas tree for the customary Nativity scene and in the giving of gifts on December 25 instead of on January 6, the Day of the Three Kings. The spread of English is also noteworthy. English has replaced French as a second language in the schools.

Despite the increased production and the apparent prosperity, Mexico has many problems to face. Although the national wealth has increased greatly, its uneven distribution has made the disparity between the incomes of the rich and poor more striking than ever before. And despite some rise in the general standard of living, over 60 percent of the population were still ill-fed, ill-housed, and ill-clothed in 1956, 40 percent were illiterate, and 46 percent of the nation's children were not going to school. A chronic inflation since 1940 has squeezed the real income of the poor, and the cost of living for workers in Mexico City has risen five times since 1939. According to the census of 1950 (published in 1955), 89 percent of all Mexican families reporting income earned less than 600 pesos a month or $69 dollars at the 1950 rate of exchange.

The great increase in agricultural production in the past twenty years has been concentrated in only two regions of the country, the north and northwest, where a new commercial agriculture based upon large private holdings, irrigation, and mechanization has developed. The great mass of the peasantry, including those in Tepoztlán, continue to work their tiny subsistence holdings with traditional backward methods. And the contrast between the old and the new agriculture in Mexico is becoming sharper: less than 1 percent of the cultivated land is worked with the aid of the country's 55,000 tractors; about 20 percent of the land is still worked by the pre-Hispanic method of cutting and burning without benefit of plow and oxen. The production of Mexico's two basic food crops, corn and beans, has managed to keep up with the rapid population growth in the past twenty years but the margin of security has been slight. In drought years Mexico has been forced to spend its precious dollars to import huge quantities of corn to feed its people.

That the Mexican economy cannot give jobs to all of its people is indicated in the fact that from 1942 to 1955 about a million and a half Mexicans came to the United States as *braceros* or temporary agricultural laborers, and this figure does not include the "wet backs" and other illegal immigration. Mexico has also become increasingly dependent on the United States tourist trade for stabilizing its economy. In 1957, over 700,000 tourists from the United States spent almost 600 million dollars in Mexico, making tourism the single largest industry in the country. The income from the tourist trade is about equal to the total Mexican federal budget.

One aspect of the standard of living which has improved very little since 1940 is housing. With a rapidly rising population and with urbanization, crowding and slum conditions in the larger cities and towns are actually getting worse. Of the 5.2 million dwellings reported in the Mexican census of 1950, 60 percent had only one room and 25 percent two rooms; 70 percent of all houses were made of adobe, wood, poles and rods, or rubble, and only 18 percent of brick and masonry. Only 17 percent had private, piped water.

The Village

How has Tepoztlán changed in the light of these national trends? In 1956 the village did not look much different from the way it looked in 1943. The plaza and market still seemed rather desolate and unprosperous; no additional buildings had been built in the center. There were no new streets or paved roads except for two long cement treads which led up a steep street to the *Posada del Tepozteco*, the new tourist resort run by an American family. More automobile and bus traffic entered the village, and trucks came in with such new items as purified water and tanks of cooking gas for the homes of the foreign colony.

Village men still carried water to their homes from the nearest fountain; women still queued up to have their corn ground at the mills. The older people looked much the same, but the clothes of the younger people were more varied, colorful, and citified. More young women had short hair and permanent waves, and one young girl wore blue jeans. The young men wore modern trousers, shirts, and jackets, and more children had shoes, sweaters, and store-bought clothes. The small shops sold more canned goods and packaged foods, mostly to the employed people who live in the center. Old women sold ready-made tortillas in the plaza. There was still no restaurant but there were more saloons. A blare of radios came from the houses and inside some homes one saw a new kerosene or Coleman stove, aluminum pots, kerosene or gasoline lamps, forks, and hand presses for shaping tortillas. At least one home had overstuffed furniture.

But many more changes have occurred than meet the eye. As a result of the population increase—from 3,500 in 1940 to approximately 4,800 in 1957—there is a shortage of housesites and housing, and Tepoztecans petitioned the local government to make available some of the nearby communal lands for new housesites. Several homes have been built on the outskirts of the village and in the surrounding *cerros*. Formerly it was not customary to rent a house; if a Tepoztecan had an extra house he would allow another villager to use it simply for the care of it. Now rental has become quite usual.

Since the late forties Tepoztlán has had a resident doctor and since 1952 a doctor from Cuernavaca who formerly practiced in the village has come once a week to see his patients. The clientele of both doctors has been increasing. In 1950, the resident doctor had an average of 75 patients a month; by 1956 the average was 160. Tepoztecans now complain about the expense of medicines and the delay caused by having prescriptions filled in Cuernavaca; the local "druggist" cannot fill prescriptions and carries few patent medicines. The village has a free federal government health clinic which cares for children and pregnant women and administers injections. About ten patients, most of them expectant mothers, come there every day. In 1955 approximately two thousand vaccinations and revaccinations were given.

The clinic and the doctor have by no means replaced the *curanderos*, however. Tepoztecans believe that doctors can cure only certain diseases, and still frequent *curanderos* for those illnesses which they attribute to *los aires*, anger, hot or cold foods, evil eye, and sorcery. Most births are still attended by the native midwives. If the doctor happens to cure an illness thought to be caused by *los aires*, this is taken as proof that the *aires* were not truly the cause. Although the villagers have substituted new terms for old concepts—for example, *los aires* are now sometimes described as tiny animals or microbes and injections are called "cleansings"—it is questionable whether this represents much of a departure from the earlier magical thinking about the causes of disease.

Like many villages in the densely populated central plateau area, Tepoztlán has not had the benefit of the great new hydroelectric and irrigation projects. Its agricultural base has remained very much the same; there has been no mechanization and no new important cash crops have been introduced. The peasants continue to work their land as before, although a few are now using some commercial fertilizer. Because the lack of change in agriculture combined with the rapidly increasing population has forced Tepoztecans to seek work in nonfarm occupations, a much lower proportion of the gainfully occupied are now peasants. The federal campaign for the preservation of the forest resources sharply reduced charcoal production in the village and many families have thereby lost a traditional source of income. Some found work as agricultural laborers on the two or three gladiola farms that have been established in Tepoztlán; others have been employed by the nearby Y.M.C.A. Many more found work in Cuernavaca or as day laborers on road construction.

The changes in the occupational structure of the village have accentuated earlier trends. The number of nonagricultural occupations increased from 26 in 1944 to 33 in 1956 and the number of people engaged in these occupations rose from 273 to 565. This increase has been accompanied by greater specialization and a decline in the role of agriculture in the total economy. In 1944, approximately 70 percent of those engaged in nonagricultural occupations also farmed; in 1956, the comparable figure was only 25 percent! Today there is a much greater participation of women in the nonagricultural occupations than formerly. Women still predominate as teachers, *curanderos,* and corn merchants, but they now are also full-time tortilla makers, dressmakers, and hairdressers. Other new occupations in the village are those of tailor, *ciruela* merchant, and milk merchant. The increase in the number of teachers has been striking—from 21 in 1944 to 101 in 1956, an indication of the growth of a middle class in the village. Whereas formerly there was a shortage of teachers in the village, there is now a shortage of teaching jobs, and 70 Tepoztecans teach in rural schools outside of the village. Other occupations that have shown a large increase in numbers are: bus line employees, from 22 to 35; barbers, from 15 to 22; butchers, from 15 to 32; and storekeepers, from 20 to 64.

The distribution of people engaged in nonagricultural occupations by barrio shows an intensification of the older pattern of concentration in the larger central barrios: La Santísima, 27 percent; Santo Domingo, 25 percent; San Miguel, 23 percent; Santa Cruz, 11 percent; San Sebastian, 8 percent; Los Reyes, 5 percent; and San Pedro, 1 percent. Similarly, 85 percent of those engaged in the new occupations come from the three central barrios. The trend toward barrio differentiation of occupations, however, has been offset by a spread of services from the central plaza to the barrios. Each barrio now has its own corn mill and at least one store. Another interesting and symptomatic change has been the rise in the number of money lenders—from about 6 in 1944 to 18 in 1956. This reflects a much greater need for cash as well as an influx of wealth.

The only occupations that have shown a decline in the number of members since 1944 are those of carpenter, *curandero, chirimitero* (flute player), maguey fiber collector, and charcoal maker. The *huehuechiques* (ceremonial barrio officers) have completely disappeared, as I predicted in my earlier study. The *chirimiteros* are being replaced by modern secular musicians. As noted earlier, the decline in charcoal making was forced on the village by the federal authorities.

The most dramatic occupational change and one which has become a major new source of income to the village is the *bracero* movement. In 1948, fewer than thirty Tepoztecans were *braceros*—that is, temporary agricultural workers in the United States; by 1957, over six hundred men had been *braceros* for periods that varied from forty-five days to over a year. This occupational change has made for other great changes in the village. In 1943, Tepoztlán suffered from an acute land shortage. Now, because in many cases the *braceros* return to the village only to rest a few months before setting out for another period in the United States, it suffers from a shortage of manpower, and many *milpas* go uncultivated. The *braceros* earn more in some months in the United States than they could earn in almost two years in the village, and many of them have invested their savings in improvements for their houses and in land and cattle. Many have brought home portable radios, mechanical toys, clothing, and cloth—the village now has four full-time tailors who are kept busy providing tailor-made pants for the villagers. Although the *bracero* movement has broadened the perspective of some Tepoztecans, who now greet American visitors with a few words of English, most of the *braceros* are isolated in work camps or on farms, speak no English, live on a Mexican diet, and on the whole learn little about the United States and its way of life. Very few learn agricultural skills that can be applied in the village.

Most of the *braceros* from Tepoztlán are young men between the ages of twenty and thirty. They come predominantly from the upper segments of the lower economic group (Group I) but also from the middle group II (see p. 37). Few come from the poorest families and fewer from the wealthier families of Group III. This is an interesting change from the pattern in the early forties when only individuals with political connections and with experience outside of the village became *braceros*. At that time most Tepoztecans feared to leave the village for a distant country or even to go to the government recruiting stations for *braceros* in Mexico City. With more education, the younger generation developed a greater readiness to explore the outside world and to dare the hazards of a long journey. The sudden spurt in *bracerismo* did not occur, however, until a school teacher in one of the outlying villages became a *bracero* recruiter (locally called *coyote*). He had been a *bracero* himself and knew how to make the necessary legal arrangements. Tepoztecan men paid him a fee in the hope that he would get them longer contracts and also jobs in California rather than in Texas or Arkansas. The fees, which the *coyote* purportedly shared with government authorities, ranged from 200 to 400 pesos depending on the length of time of work specified in the contract. Most of the villagers who signed up had to borrow from local money lenders at the usual high rate of interest but they had avoided having to deal directly with the authorities and so had found the courage to take the initial step.

The *bracero* movement has served as a partial though temporary solution of the agrarian problem in the village. Tepoztlán has become dependent on the United States economy. Were the United States suddenly to close its borders to Mexican *braceros,* there would probably be a crisis both in the village and in the nation.

Another important change in Tepoztecans is their greater readiness to sell their land. In 1943, it was difficult to find anyone in the village who would consider selling a housesite or an agricultural plot. For example, in 1942 a leading Mexican banker who wanted to build a home in the village negotiated for over a year before he succeeded in buying a modest-sized idle plot of land whose owner was living in Mexico City. By 1956, Tepoztecans had sold almost forty plots to as many outsiders for building homes in the village and in the lovely valley below. Tepoztecan middlemen are now speculating in land because of the steadily rising prices. A village site valued at about 50 centavos per square meter in 1943 sold in 1957 for as much as 12 pesos a meter (100 centavos to the peso).

Tepoztlán has become an international tourist colony. The non-Tepoztecan home owners now include native Mexicans, naturalized Mexican citizens of Spanish, French, German, Dutch, Japanese, and Italian ancestry, and a few Americans. Few of these people live in the village the year around but spend their holidays and vacations there. The construction of thirty-five new homes for the foreign colony has given employment to some Tepoztecan masons and day laborers. Some of the building materials—stone, sand, and tiles—also have been purchased locally. A number of the families have taken Tepoztecan girls as domestic servants both in the village and in their Mexico City or United States homes, and about a dozen Tepoztecans have jobs as caretakers. The colony also provides some additional income to local meat and milk dealers and other merchants. On the whole, the "foreigners" form few friendships in the village and except for the *Carnaval* participate very little in village affairs. It is said that most of the outsiders opposed the campaign to bring electricity to Tepoztlán for fear that it might spoil the primitive rustic quality of the village. It should be noted that among the non-Tepoztecans who have lived in the village are some of Mexico's leading intellectuals and artists and a few doctors. Some of these men have taken a great interest in the villagers and have helped them in their efforts to build a new high school, to obtain city water, and most recently (June 1958) to procure electricity.

Other forms of tourism have also grown rapidly and tourist facilities have improved. Most important has been the conversion of the banker's private home into one of the most charming resorts in Mexico, the *Posada del Tepozteco*. Since the late forties, Mexican and Hollywood movie producers have used Tepoztlán as the setting for a number of movies.

Since 1943, educational facilities have been expanded in the village. Two new schools built in the larger barrios gave the village a total of four elementary schools. Attendance rose from about 750 in 1950 to over 900 in 1956. In 1950, a high school was completed, and attendance rose from 54 in the first year to 110 in 1956. Boys still predominate over girls in both elementary and high schools. The surrounding villages have begun to reach out for higher education and now send their children to the central high school in Tepoztlán. Each year a number of Tepoztecan high-school graduates go on to the university in Mexico City.

In the past ten years bus travel to Cuernavaca has almost doubled and travel to Mexico City also has increased. On an average week day approximately 500 Tepoztecans take the bus to Cuernavaca to work, shop, study, sell produce, and to find recreation. Some of the peasants now think it worthwhile to take the bus to their *milpas,* a distance of two or three kilometers, rather than spend the time and energy in walking. A count made on a Wednesday in July 1956 showed that 84 vehicles entered the village and 94 left it between 5 A.M. and 9 P.M. Thirty-six percent were buses which ran about two times an hour in both directions (to and from Cuernavaca), 41 percent were passenger cars, and 23 percent were trucks. The trucks carried various products—corn, pigs, plants, beer, gravel, groceries, soft drinks, and petroleum. A similar count made on a Sunday gave a total of 373 vehicles entering and leaving. The buses carried approximately 800 passengers during the day.

In 1943, the number of radios in the village was only three or four; by 1956 it had risen to eighty, battery operated, for electricity had not yet come to the village. The owners were mainly under forty; older people showed little interest in radios. Most of them had been bought in Cuernavaca since 1950 at prices ranging from 400 to 3,500 pesos. They were intended chiefly for family use but their presence has increased visiting and sociability among the younger people. The listeners are usually not program conscious. Whenever they want to listen to something, they turn the dials to whatever sounds good. *Ranchero* music is the most popular attraction, news a secondary item. Major obstacles to the further use of radios have been lack of money and the absence of electricity, which meant trouble and expense in keeping the batteries charged. About 15 percent of the sets were not working in July 1956 because the batteries had run down. Tepoztecans who had relatives or *compadres* among bus drivers could have their batteries installed in a bus for a day and so have them charged without cost.

In 1956, as part of a federal government project to improve communications, a telephone exchange was installed in a small grocery store in Tepoztlán. Six phones were listed for the village in the Cuernavaca directory, almost all of them for local businesses. Storekeepers can now make orders, politicians can arrange meetings, and in emergencies ambulances and doctors can be reached by phone. During the day, calls are sent and received through the central office; at night, when the central office is closed, calls go to the *Posada.* The grocer charges 50 centavos to call someone to the phone, provided they live near the center of the village. During my stay in the village in 1956 a few calls from Hollywood were received by the village government—arrangements for the filming of another movie in Tepoztlán were in process!

Tepoztlán now has a movie, operated by a villager who had been a *bracero.* The movies are shown on week-ends from October to May in one of the large rooms of the municipal building which seats about 300 people. The movie business is an insecure one in Tepoztlán, however; it cannot always successfully compete with the fiestas. Most of the films are Mexican cowboy and war pictures which appeal to young people. Adults over forty do not frequent the movies and most of the peasants do not permit their daughters to attend.

Despite the higher educational level, greater travel, and the increase in radios, our data suggest that there has been no increase in the number of people who read newspapers. On the contrary, there seems to have been some decline since 1943. In 1956, only about twenty-five individuals read a newspaper with some regularity and none of them were peasants. Magazine reading has increased, however. In 1956, about fifty villagers had magazine subscriptions. About half of these were for *Selecciones,* the Spanish version of the *Readers Digest;* others were for such publications as *Life, La Granja, La Tierra, La Sevilla.* Over a third of the subscriptions were held by teachers and most of the others by persons in nonagricultural occupations. The majority of the subscribers were under fifty, and reading was predominantly done by the men. Except for school teachers and some officials, few people owned books, but many children read comics.

Related to the developments noted above are changes in every stage of the life cycle, particularly the rearing of children. Again, most of the changes are found in the middle economic group, and the following discussion of the direction of change applies mainly to this group. Changes are occurring among the tradition-oriented members of the lower groups also, but at a much slower rate.

Women still prefer to give birth on a *petate* with the help of a midwife, but a doctor is often called in for difficult cases. Many young women are rejecting some of the "Indian" customs and cures of the midwives—the food taboos, for example, the use of smoke to help labor, and the wearing of the *huipil.* Magical practices like burying the first milk or throwing it over the roof are being discarded. Because more babies are being bottle-fed, the druggist now keeps a supply of baby bottles and nipples, as well as of formula mixtures. Young women feel less need to follow such customs as sweatbaths or the forty-day postpartum seclusion before the *sacamisa.*

A definite trend toward greater child-orientedness on the part of both parents is evident. Parents tend to be more permissive and more demonstratively affectionate with their young children. More fathers can be seen on the street carrying small children and a few help a little with the children at home. The swaddling of infants has been completely abandoned as "cruel" by some mothers. Parents indulge their children more, especially the first-born, and openly show their pride in their infants by buying them toys, shoes, and attractive clothing. This is in sharp contrast with the older attitude of guarding children from the attention of others through fear of the "evil eye." Younger and more educated parents punish more lightly, permit more play, and send their children to school for as long as possible. The period of adolescence is becoming longer and more clearcut, and the time when youths are expected to contribute to the support of the family is often delayed by years of study.

Arranged marriages have completely disappeared and more couples are marrying for love. Church weddings have become more elaborate and expensive and are patterned after those of the urban middle class. Newlyweds try to set up independent households immediately after marriage or as soon as it is economically feasible to avoid the problems of living with mothers-in-law. Some young wives work as school teachers or shopkeepers, but this is still unusual. More couples are resorting to legal divorce rather than mere separation or abandonment.

A noticeable change has occurred also among the educated middle group in attitudes and values and in the quality of interpersonal relations. It is too early to tell how deeply these changes have affected the ethos and character of the villagers, but all signs point in the direction of more profound changes to follow. In 1956, Tepoztecans seemed on the whole more outgoing and friendly and less bothered by the presence of outsiders. Children were noisier and smiled more; they were as apt to run toward as away from a stranger. Indeed, they begged tourists for centavos. Small groups of unchaperoned adolescent girls laughing and talking together were not unusual sights, and occasionally a village girl might be seen walking side by side with a boy in broad daylight. In general, the villagers were more accepting of their sophisticated members and provincialism seemed to be on the wane. There was more competition for jobs and scholarships and in general display.

That Tepoztecans have more drive and ambition for self-improvement is obvious. The young people are restless and have found the courage to leave the village to look for better opportunities. They are making greater demands on their parents for education, and they have more confidence in and more ability to cooperate with people outside the family over longer periods of time. Friendship not based on formal reciprocal relationships has become increasingly important; *compadrazgo* has assumed a new significance in providing connections and social advantages. Material success and a higher standard of living are consciously admired and worked for and the motivation to hide wealth is weaker. Respect has come to be based more and more on wealth and social status. Education imparts higher status; a young man or woman who has a teacher's certificate expects to be treated more respectfully by his or her elders. The middle class, especially, feel that status is also gained by discarding folk beliefs and practices and becoming more Catholic.

It is apparent, then, that Tepoztlán has made great strides ahead in the past fifteen years. The changes have been uneven, however, and not all the sectors of the population have equally benefited. Faced with limited agricultural resources, low yields, an absence of irrigation, and little prospect of solving their agricultural problems through mechanization, the villagers have by-passed their agrarian problem and have instead become dependent on new occupations and on jobs outside the village.

Most of the changes in the village are enjoyed by the middle economic group which even in 1943 had shown the most initiative and interest in raising its level of living. This group has doubled in size and now constitutes about 25 percent of the total population. Moreover, it is no longer merely an economic group; it is emerging rather as a true middle class, consisting of professionals, white-collar employees, and self-employed artisans and shopkeepers whose values and goals have come to differ substantially from those of the peasantry. The sharpening cleavage between the middle and lower economic groups, between peasant and nonpeasant, is perhaps the most far-reaching and significant change in the village.

Although the lower economic group is proportionately smaller than it was in 1943, it still constitutes the great majority of the villagers—approximately 65 percent. Our data suggest that this group has become even poorer, both because of inflation and because its members have been deprived of a traditional source of income by the prohibiting of charcoal production. Members of the lower segments of this group have gained least from the processes set in motion by the Mexican Revolution. They have been unable or unwilling to leave the village for jobs in the cities or to work as *braceros*. They have taken least advantage of the greater educational opportunities. They continue to farm for subsistence and cling to the old ways of life largely because these are cheaper.

As Tepoztlán moves further into the modern world, it is leaving behind its Indian language, many of its Indian customs, its local autonomy and the collective forms of pre-Hispanic times. Even the communal lands—the bulwark of the traditional order and formerly one of the most important bases for the corporate life of the community—seem destined to be divided up into *ejido* plots, and perhaps later into private holdings. With improved means of communication, greater faith in technology, greater dependence on a money economy and outside jobs, increasing occupational specialization, and a desire for a higher level of living, a change has come about also in the character of the people. As we have seen, Tepoztecans are now less suspicious, less withdrawn, and more concerned with personal development.

Tepoztlán today poses many questions which can be answered only with time. Will the growing individualism bring greater anxiety and frustration? Will it bring greater participation and trust in government? Will the traditional patterns of village life be able successfully to incorporate and reinterpret the present new elements—as has often been done with new elements in the past—or will the old and stable village culture soon be unrecognizable? Will Tepoztecans continue to sell their ancient lands and thereby convert Tepoztlán into a miniature Cuernavaca? Will the recent arrival of electricity be followed by the establishment of factories and the growth of a landless proletariat? Or will the village culture absorb the industrialism that seems to be on its way as some other villages have done?

Changes in village culture are exemplified in changing styles.

Recomme...

BEALS, RALPH, 1946, *Ch...*
U.S. Government P...
An ethnograp...
state of Michoac...

FOSTER, GEORGE M., ...
Mexico: Imprenta Nuev...
A modern ethnography...
of Michoacan near Lake P...

GRUENING, ERNEST, 1928, *Mexi...*
pany.
An excellent overall history of M...
and political events since pre-Hispan...

LEWIS, OSCAR, 1951, *Life in a Mexican V...*
Ill.: University of Illinois Press.
A comprehensive description of village life...
which have occurred since Robert Redfield's...

PARSONS, ELSIE CLEWS, 1936, *Mitla, Town of the...*
of Chicago Press.
A good description of a Zapotecan Indian village o...
state of Oaxaca. Especially interesting for its chapt...
and the discussion of what is Indian and what is Spanish.

REDFIELD, ROBERT, 1930, *Tepoztlán: A Mexican Village*. Chica... ...niversity
of Chicago Press.
A pioneer study of a Mexican village especially good for the detailed
description of the fiesta cycle.

———, 1950, *A Village That Chose Progress, Chan Kom Revisited*. Chicago:
University of Chicago Press.
A study in culture change by an outstanding anthropologist who returned
for a second look to the site of one of his earlier studies.

TANNENBAUM, FRANK, 1950, *Mexico, the Struggle for Peace and Bread*. New
York: Knopf.
A concise survey of Mexico's sociology, politics, economics, and psychology
by a leading historian who has had almost three decades of familiarity
with the country.

WHETTEN, NATHAN L., 1948, *Rural Mexico*. Chicago: University of Chicago
Press.
A comprehensive description and analysis of rural Mexico which provides
an excellent background and frame of reference for the understanding of
a particular village like Tepoztlán.

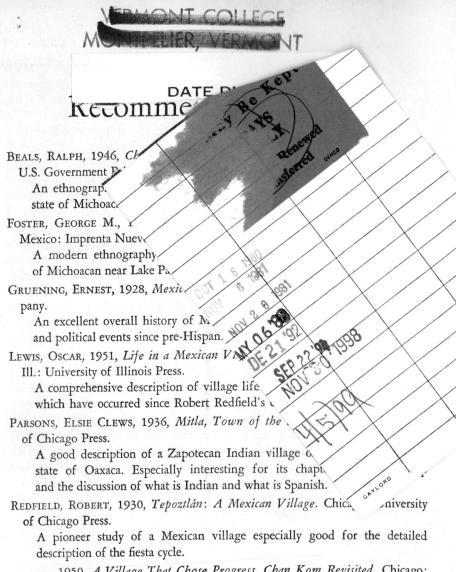